CHAUCERIAN ESSAYS

CHAUCERIAN ESSAYS

BY

GORDON HALL GEROULD

PRINCETON, NEW JERSEY
PRINCETON UNIVERSITY PRESS
1952

LONDON: GEOFFREY CUMBERLEGE, OXFORD UNIVERSITY PRESS

L.C. CARD 52-8767

PRINTED IN THE UNITED STATES OF AMERICA
BY PRINCETON UNIVERSITY PRESS AT PRINCETON, NEW JERSEY

PREFACE

THOUGH this little book is not controversial in intention, each of its chapters was written because at some time or other during the decades of what may be called my professional interest in Geoffrey Chaucer I have been irked by current interpretations or the lack of them. I have been dissatisfied with certain accepted explanations, or I have felt a need of explanation for things which by earlier readers had been taken for granted. To some of these problems I found solutions long ago and did not hide them from my pupils, graduate and undergraduate. I hope that in this way, for example, I have helped to eradicate the false notion that the pilgrims paused at an ale-house while the Pardoner took a meditative drink, but until now I have never gone on record with a proper statement about the matter. The true explanation seems to me inescapable once it is pointed out, but somehow the old error is still repeated. If former students of mine should chance to read and remember, I hope they will not think me here and elsewhere unduly repetitive. After all, I have dispensed my wares to relatively few, and novel truths—as I believe some of my ideas to be —require persuasive and reiterated statement.

My Chaucerian references are consistently to the one-volume *Poetical Works of Chaucer,* edited by F. N. Robinson, Boston, 1933.

G.H.G.

Princeton, June 1951

contents

chaucerian essays

Kalenderes enlumyned ben thei
That in this world ben lighted with thi name.

I · Chaucer's Calendar of Saints

In a versified acrostic, which we know as *An A B C*, Geoffrey Chaucer thus referred to the elaborately decorated calendars for the ecclesiastical year in which the feasts dedicated to the Virgin would of course have been marked with peculiar care. He was paraphrasing an alphabetical address to the Queen of Heaven inserted by Guillaume de Deguileville in *Le Pèlerinage de la Vie Humaine,* a poetical allegory that pleased the taste of the fourteenth century and was translated by John Lydgate in the fifteenth, though today we find it tedious. Guillaume had written that the name of the Virgin not only illumined calendars but enlightened other books whenever it appeared, and Chaucer took over the more specific reference. A calendar in which her feasts were noted, that is, needed no decorative initials, for her name was a sufficient decoration.

The notion that Chaucer was at best a Laodicean in religious feeling has in the past been fostered by some scholars who have been unable to see that an amused tolerance of the frailties of the flesh is not inconsistent with spiritual aspiration, and it has been generally held by such readers as have done no more than stumble through half a dozen of the *Canterbury Tales.* That there is no warrant for the opinion must be apparent to anyone whose eyes and ears have not been shut to the devotional intensity of the stanzas with which the Prioress prefaces her tale of the "litel clergeon," and indeed to the exquisite tenderness with which a sensational anecdote is so turned as to emphasize both the agonized passion of the earthly mother and the unfailing benignity of the Blessed Virgin. Though the attribution of the story as it stands to the gentle Prioress is very suitable, one must not forget that the shaping hand was Chaucer's.

Still more clearly, the *Invocacio ad Mariam* which forms a part of the prologue to the *Second Nun's Tale* reveals the strength of his religious faith. Here, we can be certain, the emotion was not simulated for any dramatic purpose, since in marking the poem for delivery by the Nun who attended the Prioress he did not expunge a telltale reference to himself.

> And though that I, unworthy sone of Eve,
> Be synful, yet accepte my bileve.

The magnificent prayer—one of the noblest and most beautiful passages of devotional poetry in our tongue—was Chaucer's own. That he had in conscious memory lines from the twenty-third canto of Dante's *Paradiso,* and patterned his upon them, borrowing both concepts and images, did not make what he wrote either a translation or a paraphrase. Dante's verses were refashioned or, it might be better to say, new-fashioned, shot through with echoes from hymns with which he was so familiar that the source of a particular phrase might well have been almost as elusive to him as to us. The processes of poetic composition could not be better illustrated, since the general pattern is so clearly derivative and the resulting product so genuinely original and sincerely felt. The fact that Chaucer used part of the very same passage from Dante as the basis for one stanza of the prayer put into the mouth of the Prioress, to which reference has already been made, further emphasizes the depth of its impression upon him and the value he set upon it.

If further evidence were needed to show that religion meant more to him than formal adherence to certain beliefs and practices, it might be pointed out that a man so occupied with many things as we know him to have been would scarcely have taken the time, unless impelled by stern convictions, to translate or compile the treatise on penance and the mortal sins which we call the *Parson's Tale*. The notion that because he lived in the fourteenth century rather than the nineteenth or the twentieth he might perform such labors without serious intent does not bear scrutiny. In no age could they have been done by inadvertence. Even though the content of the *Parson's Tale* and the *Boece* is not of Chaucer's devising, he made both works his own; and the *Consolations* of the Christian philosopher awaiting the end of life were so woven into the fabric of his mind that echoes of them are scattered throughout his poetry in much the same degree as are the very different borrowings from the *Roman de la Rose*.

It might be possible to argue, though a little speciously, that the great frequency of allusions and images drawn from the Scriptures and service-books means little as to Chaucer's personal feeling, since his memory would inevitably have been stored with what he had heard over and over again since childhood. Taken in connection, however, with his explicitly devotional poetry and prose, the allusions and images have importance. What he used consciously interprets his feeling about what came unsummoned from his memory to enrich the texture of his poetry. We of another age may be permitted to regret that in the Retractation appended to the *Parson's Tale*—but composed when or how we cannot know—he was impelled to ask forgiveness for having written some of his works of highest seriousness; but we must not on that account think that religious devotion was fugitive and evanescent with him.

> Thow Mayde and Mooder, doghter of thy Sone,
> Thow welle of mercy, synful soules cure,
> In whom that God for bounte chees to wone,

Thow humble, and heigh over every creature,
Thow nobledest so ferforth oure nature,
That no desdeyn the Makere hadde of kynde
His Sone in blood and flessh to clothe and wynde.

The man who wrote that stanza and the ones which follow it was a true believer as well as a great poet.

Nor can the uncompleted work which Chaucer once referred to as the *Seintes Legende of Cupide* and once as the *Book of the XXV Ladies* be adduced as evidence of disrespect for the heroes and heroines of the Church. Legends were tales of devotion, and were to be accepted in a devotional spirit. No question about the historic validity of the events related would have troubled the mind of any medieval reader. One did not approach them with critical sensibilities awake, for the truth of them lay in the justice with which they mirrored some of the loftiest aspirations of the human heart. One can be playful about sacred things only if one thoroughly believes them, for there is then no flippancy in the playfulness. To say that the *Legend of Good Women* is a burlesque or parody would be a gross misstatement, though Chaucer modelled his collection on the legendaries and pretended that the faithful ladies he celebrated were the martyrs of love. What he could do as a parodist, which is something very different, he showed in *Sir Thopas*.

Chaucer's own calendar of saints, as we may call it, was of course uncalculated and unarranged. His references are for the most part casual, and in very many instances have no importance whatever beyond showing that the names came naturally to mind. Such familiarity they do show, even when they occur only as oaths. Introduced as they are in various ways and on various occasions, they might be expected to be fairly representative: the names of saints well known to the cultivated layman of the period. A survey of them shows the reasonableness of this expectation, but it shows also a few oddities, for some of which no adequate explanation has as yet been found.

All in all, if we exclude from consideration the *Parson's Tale* as being a translated work, Chaucer refers to forty-two saints by name. In addition, seven places of pilgrimage are mentioned, five of them without specifying the sacred relics or the persons celebrated at the shrines. These are the five which the Wife of Bath is said to have visited: Boulogne, Rome, Compostella, Cologne, and Jerusalem; and to Jerusalem she had journeyed thrice.[1] There is dramatic propriety in making the Reeve, a Norfolk man, allude to Bromholm,[2] since the priory of that name with its cross reputedly fashioned from the wood of the True Cross and brought back by a crusading priest early in the thirteenth century was in that county; but it is not so evident why the wife of a Cambridgeshire miller should appeal in her terror to the same holy relic. Clearly, however, Chaucer knew much better than we can know what words it was right for the Reeve to put in her mouth. Another allusion equally lacking in reverence is that to the phial which Edmund of Cornwall presented in 1270 to the Premonstratensian Abbey of Hales, or Hales-Owen, in Shropshire, the legend being that it contained a portion of Christ's blood brought to Rome by Titus and Vespasian, and thence to Treves by Charlemagne. The Pardoner, it will be recalled, gives sharp emphasis to his reproof of "fals sweryng" by dramatically representing a quarrel at hazard. "By the blood of Christ that is in Hayles," one of the players is made to exclaim.[3]

Certain other references varying in kind illustrate Chaucer's consciousness of the saints and their legends as well as the general familiarity of everyone with all such matters.

[1] *CT*, I,463-466. (A table of abbreviations used for Chaucer's works and for journal and text references will be found at the back of the book.)

[2] *CT*, I,4286.

[3] *CT*, VI,652.

In the *Canon's Yeoman's Tale,* for example, the foolish priest who is being bamboozled by the Canon invokes for him the blessing of God, the Virgin, and "alle halwes."[4] Three times in the *Canterbury Tales* there is mention of the Trinity, twice in oaths[5] and once towards the close of the *Prioress's Tale* when the abbot appeals to the murdered boy to tell them "in vertu of the hooly Trinitee" why he still sings his antiphon though his throat is cut.[6] Two allusions in *Troilus and Criseyde* emphasize by their very anachronism how natural it was for Chaucer to think of saints and their cults, whatever the matter in hand. In the course of the gay interchange of pleasantries between Pandarus and Criseyde when he first waits on her in behalf of Troilus, she repels his proposal of a dance by saying that as a widow,[7]

> It sate me wel bet ay in a cave
> To bidde and rede on holy seyntes lyves.

Very different is the poignant cry with which Troilus ends his lament before the desolate and empty palace of Criseyde while he still hopes for her return:[8]

> And farwel shryne, of which the seynt is oute!

And finally, the statement about Lucrece in the *Legend of Good Women* is an intentional transference from paganism to Christianity, since "in hir lawe"

> she was holden there
> A seynt, and ever hir day yhalwed dere.[9]

There is no possibility, admittedly, of finding out what service-books Chaucer owned, or the calendar with which he was most familiar. His experience of places as well as of men was very wide. It is interesting to observe, neverthe-

4 *CT,* VIII,1244.
5 *CT,* III,1824, V,682.
6 *CT,* VII,646.
7 *T&C,* II,117-118.
8 *T&C,* V,553.
9 *LGW,* lines 1870-1871.

less, that of the forty-two saints whom he mentions in one passage or another all but seven appear in the calendar of a Westminster missal written between 1362 and 1386.[10] The days observed by a great foundation at the very heart of the kingdom would at least have been noticed by a courtier and public servant like Chaucer, and they constituted a traditionally normal list.

Of the seven names lacking in the Westminster calendar two are absurdities perpetrated by Harry Bailly. In both instances we can only guess what saints he can be supposed to have had in mind. What was "that precious corpus Madrian" by which he swore in commending the tale of *Melibeus*?[11] A St. Maternus was suggested long ago; but there is no evidence that either the fourth century bishop of Cologne and Treves or the slightly earlier bishop of Milan was ever known in England. Neither name appears in Bede's calendar or in any later one. Nor is St. Maturinus, or Mathurin, a wholly satisfactory candidate. He was an obscure figure of perhaps the fourth century, not recorded in any English calendar, though his burial place near Sens won at least regional celebrity during the later medieval centuries. The legend came to be that at the end of life Mathurin was called to Rome to free the emperor's daughter from the power of an evil spirit, and that his body would not remain buried until it was brought back to France. Although this story, with its emphasis on a "precious corpus" appears in the Caxton translation of *Legenda Aurea,* it is not found in the generally accepted Latin text, which omits any mention of the saint. Unless Chaucer at some time learned about the legend in Paris, where two churches were dedicated to St. Mathurin, it seems unlikely that "Madrian" is a distortion of his name. A better guess is that the name stands for St. Medardus, or Medard, a widely celebrated

[10] *Missale ad usum Ecclesie Westmonasteriensi,* ed. J. W. Legge, 1892-1897.

[11] *CT,* VII,1892.

bishop of Noyon and Tournai who died towards the middle of the sixth century. His remains were translated in great pomp from Noyon to Soissons, where they became the "precious corpus" of a famous Benedictine monastery. In England his name is found in all calendars from Bede's onward, and at least one church was dedicated to him.[12]

The other saint's name corrupted by Harry Bailly is even more troublesome. He swears by "seint Ronyan" while praising the Physician for his tale, and is mockingly echoed by the Pardoner immediately thereafter.[13] The copyists, who were content with "Madrian" and never varied the spelling, were sadly puzzled by his other oath and gave the name eighteen different forms,[14] some of them so widely different as quite evidently to be conscious substitutions, while modern editors, with good manuscript authority, have varied the spelling of the final syllable to make it rhyme first with "man" and then with "anon." To state, as Skeat does, that the forms "are evidently corruptions of Ronan, a saint whose name is well known to readers of *St. Ronan's Well*," in nowise clarifies the matter, since it then becomes necessary to identify an extremely elusive St. Ronan. The Bollandists enumerate[15] no less than seven saints under the name Romanus and two named Ronanus, as well as a Romualdus, a Romoldus, and a Rumwoldus. It is not surprising that the names and festivals of these twelve persons have been confused. Only Romanus of August 9 and Romanus of October 23 appear in the calendars of Sarum and Westminster, but a Ronanus is found in calendars of Canterbury,[16] while Irish calendars list several others.[17]

12 The suggestion of G. L. Frost, *MLN*, LVII (1942), 177-179, that the Host confused *madrian*, a condiment, with a saint's name is ingenious but implausible.

13 *CT*, VI, 310, 320.

14 Computed on the basis of Manly and Rickert, *CT*, VII.

15 *Bibliotheca hagiographica latina* and Supplement.

16 See F. A. Gasquet and E. Bishop, *The Bosworth Psalter*, 1908, p. 115.

17 *ibid.*, pp. 177-178; and C. Plummer, *Venerabilis Baedae Historiam Ecclesiasticam*, 1896, II, 188.

The saints listed in the English calendars just mentioned are not, however, those with similar names to whom church dedications can be attributed. According to the two chief authorities on such dedications, a St. Rumon (June 1) appears four times,[18] he being entered by the Bollandists as Ronanus, while there are either seven[19] or eight[20] dedications to St. Rumwaldus, whose name is otherwise spelled Rumbald, Rumwald, and Romald. Only in the calendar of Sion Monastery have I noted the name thus variously spelled,[21] that of a holy infant whose popularity is attested by the widely scattered dedications by which he was honored. To add to the general confusion, the name of St. Ninian, as noted by Professor Robinson, was frequently corrupted to something not very different from the forms just mentioned. "In vulgar Scotch he was S. Ringan or S. Ringen," says the editor of his life.[22] "In the north of England a further debasement occurs, in the forms of S. Trinyon and S. Triman." Still other variants are recorded in a study of Scottish holy wells: Ringald and Ronan.[23] St. Ninian also appears in the Sion calendar as Mynyane.[24]

It is evident that we shall never know what saint Chaucer meant Harry Bailly to have had in mind when he swore by St. Ronyan. If the evidence of the manuscripts is valid, however, and the Pardoner was made to vary the final syllable intentionally, the suggestion of Tupper a generation

18 F. Arnold-Forster, *Studies in Church Dedications,* 1899, II,116, III,445, and F. Bond, *Dedications and Patron Saints of English Churches,* 1914, p. 19.

19 Arnold-Forster, I,174, III,445.

20 Bond, p. 19.

21 *The Martiloge in Englysshe,* ed. F. Procter and E. S. Dewick, 1893, p. 173.

22 A. P. Forbes, *Lives of S. Ninian and S. Kentigern,* 1874, p. 256.

23 J. R. Walker, *Proceedings of the Society of Antiquaries in Scotland,* New Ser., V (1883),199-201.

24 Procter and Dewick, p. 147. The detailed and erudite argument for Ninian by J. Sledd, *Med. Studies,* XIII (1951),226-233, fails to settle the matter.

ago, that he was perpetrating a ribald pun[25] may perhaps be true. *Runnion,* with more than one scabrous meaning, is close in sound to *Ronyon.* Yet one a little hesitates to accept the explanation in view of the confusion of the fifteenth-century scribes. Evidently they failed to understand the joke if joke there was.

Apart from the strange oaths of Harry Bailly, five other saints' names are mentioned by Chaucer which do not appear in the Westminster list. Their omission is not difficult to explain. The legend of Longinus, though widely popular and included in various medieval martyrologies, belonged like all stories from the Apocryphal Gospels in a very doubtful category. Ecclesiastical authority had been unable in earlier centuries to suppress those picturesque works, and the legends lived on unauthorized because of their intrinsic interest as stories. Chaucer's acquaintance with the legend is shown by his insertion of the name Longius[26] in *An A B C,* though the poem by Deguilleville which he was translating has no such reference.

That the names of St. Bernard of Clairvaux and St. Clare had not been entered in a Benedictine calendar of the later fourteenth century is not surprising, since their cults were primarily the concern of the Cistercians and the Franciscans respectively. Yet Chaucer would inevitably have known about them. His references, to Bernard as the subject of a proverb[27] and to Clare in an oath uttered by the resplendent eagle of the *House of Fame,*[28] bear witness to their general fame.

No process of canonization, it is needless to say, was ever undertaken for the Hugh of Lincoln to whom the affecting

[25] F. Tupper, *JEGP,* xv (1916),66. Tupper was surely wrong in thinking the Host a party to the jest.

[26] *ABC,* line 163.

[27] *LGW,* line 16. See R. M. Smith, *MLN,* LX (1946),38-44, and M. P. Hamilton, *MLN,* LXI (1947),192-193.

[28] *HF,* line 1066.

apostrophe is addressed at the end of the *Prioress's Tale*,[29] and his name would have appeared in no official list. Reputedly murdered in 1255 ("but a litel while ago"), he had acquired by Chaucer's day such popular fame that the Prioress, and perhaps the poet himself, would have accepted the story as historically true. Nor did the Church's failure to approve the legend keep it from being remembered. People have been singing a ballad about it even in the present century.

The probability that the Host had St. Medard in mind when he swore by "that precious corpus Madrian" is at least slightly increased by Chaucer's reference elsewhere to two other saints whose cults likewise developed in the region of Noyon and Tournai. The first of these was Godeleva, styled in French Godelième or Godeleine, who was murdered, according to the legend, at the command of her brutal husband about 1070. "Goode Lief," an expletive used by the Wife of Bath in reporting her treatment of her earlier husbands, certainly refers, as has recently been shown by Miss Seaton,[30] to this pious and unfortunate lady, whose martyrdom for the faith was recognized by the Bishop of Noyon as early as 1088. The Host's use of the name to designate his vixenish wife[31] was a stroke of irony, since the two lives of the saint emphasize her wifely patience.

St. Eligius, finally, a bishop of Noyon in the seventh century, is not included in the Westminster calendar. This would be very surprising in view of his great fame on the Continent, were it not that his name is omitted from most other such lists.[32] Yet there is sufficient evidence, apart from Chaucer's two allusions, that he was widely known

[29] *CT*, VII,684. [30] *CT*, III,431. See E. Seaton, *MLR*, XLI (1946),196-202.

[31] *CT*, VII,1894. Miss Rickert and others had earlier recognized that Goodelief was a not uncommon personal name in Kent.

[32] See F. Wormald, *English Benedictine Calendars after 1100*, 1939, II,102. At St. Neot's, a cell of Bec, where the calendar included him, he was celebrated on June 25 rather than December 1.

on the English side of the Channel. As every reader of the Prologue to the *Canterbury Tales* remembers, it is said of the Prioress[33] that

> Hire gretteste ooth was but by Seinte Loy.

Later, in the *Friar's Tale*,[34] the carter who innocently assists the Devil to the discomfiture of the Summoner calls upon the saint to aid his struggling horse, and the haywagon is thereupon released from the mire.

The incongruity of these two references suggests the oddities of the legend which developed about the figure of an important bishop of the French church. That he should have been venerated as an artist and the special patron of artificers in metal and enamel was quite in accord with the biography which purported to be the work of his friend St. Ouen and indeed was probably based on a contemporary account by him.[35] That he should have become the patron of carters and farriers is a strange quirk of popular lore for which there is nothing in the earlier record to account, not even the story of a horse so devoted to the bishop that it fell sick when wrongfully seized by another bishop after its master's death.[36] To the evidence presented or alluded to by Lowes in an admirable study of the legend[37] may be added a few items which show that in Great Britain as well as on the Continent the later fame of the saint was based on his reputed skill in dealing with horses. The iconographical representations of him which have been found[38] show

[33] *CT*, I,120.

[34] *CT*, III,1564.

[35] The opinion of B. Krusch, whose edition of the *Vita* is found in *MGH, Script. Rerum Merovingicarum*, IV (1902),634-761, and of A. Poncelet, *Analecta Bollandiana*, XXII (1903),108-109.

[36] I can find no evidence for the statement of Baring-Gould, *Lives, sub* Eligius, that the shift came about through a misunderstanding of the word *sella*, throne, by "mediaeval artists" who "rendered this a saddle and made of Eligius a farrier." It is true that *sellarius* meant saddler in the thirteenth century.

[37] J. L. Lowes, *Romanic Review*, V (1914),368-385.

[38] See Bond, *op.cit.*, p. 156.

him with a horseshoe, while Sir David Lyndsay, listing in *Experience and ane Courteour* the images of saints familiar to him, refers to Sanct Eloye[39] with

> Ane new hors schoo in tyll his hand.

In the following section of the poem, which deprecates the practice of appealing to the saints for help, Lyndsay says:[40]

> Sum makis offrande to Sanct Eloye,
> That he there hors may weill convoye.

By Chaucer's time Eligius must have been quite generally known in England even though his day was little celebrated and though only four dedications of churches have been traced.[41]

The popular repute of the saint as the patron of farriers and carters, which so distorted the earlier legend, helps in no way to an understanding of Chaucer's enigmatic reference to the oath of the Prioress. Nor is there anything in the earlier legend which satisfactorily explains what Chaucer meant. The theory that the oath was no oath at all has been properly discarded, while the conclusions of Lowes, which have won general acceptance, are open to question on two or three counts. First of all, he assumed without trying to define them "considerations" that "kept the Prioress from invocation of the greater saints." But the fact is that Eligius cannot be regarded as a saint of little importance any more than can be St. Germanus or St. Martin or St. Remigius.

Furthermore, there is nothing in Chaucer's line to indicate that the Prioress was "kept" from invoking other saints. May it not be that her greatest oath was *only* by St. Eloy because she had for some reason a peculiar veneration

39 *Poetical Works*, ed. D. Laing, 1871, I,311.

40 *ibid.*, I,314.

41 Arnold-Forster, *op.cit.*, I,475; Bond, *op.cit.*, p. 23. Bond in giving the number as one reckons only the church now existing.

for him? The history and personality of the great bishop, which Lowes rightly stressed as likely to have impressed the Prioress, may have made him the center of a cult in which she shared, even though his festival was not commonly observed by the English church. The greatest oath of the Prioress would then be by the saint to whom she owed special devotion. The fact discovered by Miss Edith Rickert that the Countess of Pembroke of Chaucer's day gave an image of St. Loy to the high altar of the Grey Friars suggested to Manly the possibility of a cult of the saint at court.[42] It is equally possible, I think, that a devotion to St. Eligius was cultivated in such establishments as St. Leonard's, Bromley, to which the Prioress clearly belonged. There has perhaps been too little stress on the activity of St. Eloy as the founder of important convents for women, first in Paris and later in Noyon. That fact, together with his eminent virtues and graces, might well have led nuns of any era to hold him in special esteem. Yet when all is said, Chaucer's line about the oath of the Prioress remains a puzzle.

The thirty-five saints mentioned by Chaucer whose names appear in the Westminster list represent fairly enough a casual sprinkling from such a calendar as a well-lettered man of the period might carry in his memory. Eight of them are British. The Cambridge student John in the *Reeve's Tale,* who was born "fer in the north," appropriately swears by St. Cuthbert;[43] and the Oxford carpenter in the *Miller's Tale* with equal propriety appeals to St. Frideswide, the virgin patroness of his city.[44] There is less good reason why Gerveys in the same tale should point his ribaldry with the name of the shadowy St. Neot.[45] As for

[42] J. M. Manly, *Some New Light on Chaucer,* 1926, p. 214, and *Canterbury Tales,* 1928, p. 505.

[43] *CT,* I,4127.

[44] *CT,* I,3449.

[45] *CT,* I,3771. See W. H. Stevenson, *Asser's Life of King Alfred,* 1904, pp. 256-261, 296-299, for the most satisfactory unravelling of tangled evidence about the saint that has been accomplished.

the equally obscure St. Yve, Chaucer would have been very familiar with the Benedictine priory in Huntingdonshire dedicated to him, and may well have been thinking rather more of that foundation than of the saint himself when he twice used the phrase "by that lord that clepid is Seint Yve," ascribing it both to the Friar in the *Summoner's Tale* and to the Merchant in the *Shipman's Tale*.[46] The Persian missionary who helped to convert the English in the seventh century was the vaguest of figures, but the priory was a solid fact as was the other St. Ives in Cornwall.

The lives or episodes from the lives of four other British saints are referred to in the *Canterbury Tales*. The Fiend in the *Friar's Tale*, when describing to the Summoner the activities of himself and other devils, remarks:

> And somtyme be we servant unto man,
> As to the erchebisshop Seint Dunstan.[47]

This allusion, which has never been explained, I believe, must derive from a story about the saint while he was a young monk at Glastonbury.[48] His earliest biographer, whom we know only as B, says of him that some young kinsmen through envy accused him of cultivating the poetry and pagan charms of antiquity, and so drove him from court.[49] By the time of Osbern, who wrote his account about a century later, the accusation had become—perhaps justifiably—more serious, since it followed the miraculous

[46] *CT*, III,1943, VII,227. The note of F. N. Robinson on the latter passage, to the effect that St. Yvo of Brittany "would also naturally have been known to Chaucer" is clearly an error. St. Yvo (1253-1303), though a learned man with a regional reputation for legal acumen as well as holiness, never became famous outside the province. He remained a parish priest in the diocese of Tréguier throughout his life, and could not appropriately be referred to as "that lord." Robinson's "third saint, a twelfth-century bishop of Chartres," was never made a saint, though he was beatified. Miss Ruth H. Cline, *MLN*, LX (1945),482, failed to observe this.

[47] *CT*, III,1501-1502.

[48] Sister Mary Immaculata, *PQ*, XXI (1942), though she examined the successive lives of Dunstan, failed to note the story.

[49] *Memorials of St. Dunstan*, ed. W. Stubbs, 1874, p. 11.

playing of his harp while he was employed in designing a stole. The king was told that Dunstan was initiated in evil arts and was aided by demons.[50] A third biographer, Eadmer, a few years afterward, limited the accusation somewhat, specifying that the miraculous harp-playing was arranged with devilish aid.[51] Osbern's form of the story was taken over in the collection of legends compiled in the fourteenth century by John of Tynemouth.[52] The devil of the *Friar's Tale,* it will be seen, was merely asserting for himself a relationship traditionally attributed to him by others. Since Chaucer's reference is so casual, one is inclined to believe that he had somewhere heard or read the story in the form he gives it; but I have been unable to find such a version.

When the Monk good-naturedly agrees to tell "a tale, or two, or three," and to recite the "lyf of Seint Edward,"[53] we may safely assume that he meant the story of Edward the Confessor. He chooses, however, to begin with a series of "tragedies," and he refuses to go on to something else when he has been interrupted in his flow of cheerless anecdote.

Chauntecleer in the *Nun's Priest's Tale* commends to Pertelote the legend of St. Kenelm,[54] and wishes she had read it as he has done. In eleven lines he summarizes for her benefit the essential points in the story of the little Mercian prince who was warned in a dream of his approaching martyrdom. Chauntecleer may be supposed to have found the legend in the collection of John of Tynemouth, since his ostentatious pedantry would hardly have permitted him to read the widely circulated version in English.

It is a little odd that St. Thomas Becket, finally, whose name is inseparably associated with Chaucer's because of the Canterbury pilgrimage, should have been mentioned

[50] *ibid.*, p. 81.
[51] *ibid.*, p. 171.
[52] *ibid.*, p. 328, and C. Horstmann, *Nova Legenda Anglie,* 1901, I,275.
[53] *CT,* VII,1970.
[54] *CT,* VII,3110-3121.

by him so casually. Five times the name Thomas is used in oaths,[55] but in three of the instances Thomas the Apostle might well be the saint intended. The Host invokes the blessing of the English St. Thomas on the pilgrims when making his proposals to them as to the journey, and at the Watering of St. Thomas he starts the story-telling.[56] Except in the famous lines[57] at the beginning of the General Prologue, there is no other allusion to the "hooly blisful martir" or to his shrine. One wonders whether Chaucer, if he had completed his design, might not have recorded some impression of medieval Canterbury and its great abbey.

Once, and once only, as every reader knows, he told the story of a saint at length. The legend of St. Cecilia, which we know as the *Second Nun's Tale,* was composed, we have already seen, without any thought of the Prioress's "chaplain" in mind. It was Chaucer's own, though a translation faithful in substance and meaning to the rather bald and uninspired Latin prose version which was his source.[58] Out of this material he made a poem of exquisite tone and temper. It should be noted that another saint, Pope Urban, has his place in the story.

Apart from the summary of the legend of Kenelm, already mentioned, the *Prioress's Tale* has a passing reference to St. Nicholas of Myra as an instance of infant piety,[59] inasmuch as he observed the fasts of Wednesday and Friday while still nursing at the breast. A similarly passing reference to the miraculous nourishment of Mary of Egypt is found in the *Man of Law's Tale;*[60] and equally brief is an allusion in the *Summoner's Tale*[61] to St. Thomas the

55 *HF,* line 1131; *CT,* I,3291,3425,3461, III,666.

56 *CT,* I,770 and I,826 respectively.

57 *CT,* I,15-18.

58 See my study in *Sources and Analogues of Chaucer's Canterbury Tales,* ed. Bryan and Dempster, 1941, pp. 667-684.

59 *CT,* VII,514-515.

60 *CT,* II,500-501.

61 *CT,* III,1980. Robinson's note on this line is inaccurate, since the ab-

Apostle as a builder of churches while spreading the Gospel in India.

The name of St. Valentine is introduced after a somewhat different fashion from that of any other in the list we are reviewing. It appears three times: once in the *Complaint of Mars*[62] and twice in the *Parliament of Fowls*.[63] In all three instances the customs which had grown up about the festival of the saint rather than anything proper to the legend itself are the matters in question. They have to do with the belief or assumption that on St. Valentine's Day birds choose their mates for the year, as human beings at least pretend to do. Valentine himself is a vague figure, so vague that it has even been difficult to determine whether he should be counted as one person or two. The traditional belief that two centers of cult in Rome, both with feasts on February 14, implied two saints with the same name has yielded to the view that for some undiscoverable reason one Valentine was split into two.[64] The brief accounts of him[65] are wholly conventional and give no clue to the origin of the beliefs and practices later associated with his name. For the notion, frequently repeated, that the Church fostered secular celebrations on February 14th to replace the Roman Lupercalia of the day following there is no evidence whatever.[66] We know nothing about any such customs until late in the Middle Ages, and then hear of them in countries

breviated version of the story in *Legenda Aurea* omits the statement about church building. The full text may be found in M. Bonnet, *Supplementum Codicis Apocryphi I, Acta Thomae*, 1883, p. 141. Skeat notes correctly the reference in the *South-English Legendary*. The Merchant swears by Thomas of India, *CT*, IV,1230.

62 Lines 13-14.

63 Lines 309-311 and 683.

64 See H. Delehaye, *Analecta Bollandiana*, XLVII (1929),143.

65 *ASS*, Feb. II,757-763.

66 Apparently first suggested by Francis Douce, *Illustrations of Shakespeare*, 1837, II,252-258, and still repeated in spite of the sensible remarks of J. W. Hales in the best general treatment the legend has yet received: *The Antiquary*, V (1882),41-50.

across the Alps, never in Italy. That an obscure Roman saint of the third century should have gained a place in the northern calendars, as he did in England from the first, is not very surprising; but it is curious and difficult to explain that his name should have emerged after many centuries as the focus of such a widespread cult. It is worth noting that in England at least no churches are recorded to have been dedicated to him.[67]

How the popular interest in him was first aroused and when it began are probably insoluble questions. It has manifested itself in curiously different ways. In Northern France, Belgium, and England the festival became associated with the choice of lovers and the exchange of gifts. In Germany, on the other hand, to which the popular cult just mentioned seems never to have extended, the saint was appealed to for help by epileptics and by farmers with sick cattle.[68] Some trace of the German belief may possibly have become current in England, since Burton in the *Anatomy of Melancholy*, when enumerating the saints whose aid was asked by those variously afflicted, referred to "Valentine for the falling-sickness."[69] The learned Burton, however, may have been alluding to continental rather than English custom, as is certainly true of the translation by Barnaby Googe in the previous century.[70]

The tradition in France and England reflected by Chaucer and such contemporaries as Granson followed a far more interesting if equally inexplicable course.[71] Although there is no direct evidence before the end of the fourteenth century for the association of the saint with the plighting of lovers, the customs are so widespread and various within

67 Arnold-Forster, *op.cit.*, I,519-520.

68 See P. Sartori, *Sitte und Brauch*, 1910-1914, III,88; Hales, *op.cit.*, p. 41.

69 II,1,3.

70 Cited by Hales, *op.cit.*, p. 41.

71 The fullest account of English customs may be found in A. R. Wright and T. E. Lones, *British Calendar Customs*, 1936-1940, II,136-140.

the territories specified that the practice of exchanging vows and gifts on Valentine's Day may well run much farther back. That the choosing of mates and the giving of presents sometimes took place on the first of May, probably means that such customs had long been established without reference to any particular saint.[72] Another reason for believing them to have been of long standing is their absorption by the fable of the conclave of birds.[73] The combination of the two themes, which first appeared in the thirteenth century, became a literary fashion before 1400 and so influenced to some extent, no doubt, the popular customs and beliefs of later generations. The pattern was useful to Chaucer inasmuch as it enabled him to treat a very serious matter in the *Parliament of Fowls* with graceful delicacy. Quite apart from any political reference, the poem does not lack meaning.

How troublesome a casual allusion can be is well illustrated by the story of a pilgrim to the shrine of St. Leonard which Chaucer made in the opening scene of the *House of Fame*.[74] On the evening of December 10th, he says, he found himself overcome with sleep:

> As he that wery was forgo
> On pilgrymage myles two
> To the corseynt Leonard,
> To make lythe of that was hard.

Skeat's downright statement in his note that "Chaucer follows Jean de Meun" has always been accepted without question, as far as I am aware. Yet a careful comparison of the lines cited from the *Roman de la Rose*[75] must bring conviction, I think, that they are quite unrelated.

72 See F. Rabelais, *Oeuvres*, ed. A. Lefranc, 1931, v,77n.

73 For a good general treatment, see W. Seelmann, "Die Vogelsprachen," *Jahrbuch des Vereins für niederdeutsche Sprachforschung*, XIV (1888),101-147.

74 Lines 115-118.

75 Ed. Langlois, lines 8833-8838.

Mariages est maus liens
Ainsinc m'aïst sainz Juliens,
Qui pelerins erranz herberge,
E sainz Lienarz, qui desferge
Les prisoniers bien repentanz,
Quant les veit a sei dementanz.

This means, I take it, that St. Leonard releases from their bonds such prisoners as are penitent and very miserable.[76] Among the many miracles attributed to the saint the only one in which repentance is stressed, as far as I can discover, is the story of Hugues and Guillaume.[77] The latter knight, having captured Hugues in battle, imprisons him in an oubliette, from the edge of which he mocks his foe, pretending that he is St. Leonard but refusing to rescue the miserable wretch. Thereupon the saint himself intervenes, and Hugues is set free. Guillaume in consternation makes a treaty of peace with his enemy, but unfortunately does not live up to all his agreements. In the war which ensues he is captured in turn, and from his dungeon calls with true penitence on St. Leonard for aid. He is then set free by the saint. This tale may well have been remembered by Jean de Meun when he was playing with the idea of marriage as imprisonment.

But the story alluded to by Chaucer has nothing to do with a rescue from captivity. Whatever happened took place during a pilgrimage—an exceedingly short pilgrimage—of two miles to the shrine of St. Leonard. Professor Smyser has shown[78] that there is every reason to believe that Chaucer had in mind St. Leonard's, Bromley, a nunnery which stood about two miles from Aldgate, where he was living when he wrote the *House of Fame*. The pilgrim

[76] Skeat's interpretation of "dementanz" as "recalling their word" seems to me unjustifiable. Certainly Godefroy gives no warrant for it.

[77] See F. Arbellot, *Vie de St. Léonard*, 1863, pp. 82-84.

[78] H. M. Smyser, *MLN*, LVI (1941), 205-207.

was "forgo" during this brief progress, which probably means that he became very weary. Skeat's suggestion that he might have been walking "under difficulties, such as going barefoot for penance" may quite possibly be correct. But what is meant by the saying "to make the hard easy"? The line is completely enigmatic. I can find nothing in the various surviving accounts of pilgrimages to the shrine of the saint which offers any clue.[79] I fear we must accept Professor Smyser's statement that the "true purport of the allusion would probably have been clear only to Chaucer's circle." It is well to remember the great popularity of St. Leonard, in whose honor approximately one hundred and fifty English churches were dedicated as well as several monastic establishments.[80]

Though Chaucer alluded many times to the attributes and teachings of the saints, as we shall see, he directly quoted only three of them, and those three only in passages of translation. This is true of St. Ambrose's tribute to St. Cecilia[81] as well as of the sententious utterances of St. Augustine and St. Jerome in the *Melibeus*.[82] More revealing is the allusion in the *Legend of Good Women*[83] to St. Augustine's compassion for Lucrece, which derives, if perhaps through one intermediary, from *De Civitate Dei*. There is, besides, the reference to a monastic rule attributed to Augustine—"as Austyn bit"—in the description of the Monk in the General Prologue of the *Canterbury Tales*.[84]

[79] The fullest collection is that printed by Arbellot.

[80] See Arbellot, *op.cit.*, p. 213, and Arnold-Forster, *op.cit.*, II,112.

[81] *CT*, VIII,271-283.

[82] *CT*, VII,1595,1618,1640.

[83] *LGW*, lines 1690-1691. Robinson's note on "the grete Austyn" and "oure legende" needs some correction, since he failed to notice that the account of Augustine in *Legenda Aurea* begins with an elaborate play with the name and states that "sicut Augustus praecellebat omnes reges, sic et iste excellit omnes doctores." The passage thus furnishes a slight but definite piece of corroborative evidence as to Chaucer's knowledge of Jacobus.

[84] *CT*, I,187.

That the monk of the *Shipman's Tale* invokes the blessing of the same saint on his friend the merchant, and that the Host in praising the tale uses the name in an oath,[85] merely emphasize the pervasive influence of the great bishop. St. Jerome's name appears in one other passage. The antifeminist book owned by Jankyn, the fifth husband of the Wife of Bath, included Jerome's *Epistola adversus Joviniianum*,[86] a treatise from which Chaucer quarried and paraphrased without acknowledgment a considerable part of the reflections on marriage uttered by the stalwart and experienced woman.

In the description of the Monk alluded to above, he is said to have disapproved of the "reule of seint Maure or of seint Beneit" on the ground that it was old and somewhat strict.[87] The allusion to St. Benedict, whose foundation of Monte Cassino in the sixth century set the pattern for monasticism in the western church, requires no comment. The principles he laid down prevailed everywhere as the basis for all subsequent rules. The allusion to St. Maurus, on the other hand, is in dire need of explanation, though no one has hitherto attempted it. All commentators apparently have accepted without question the reference to St. Maurus as the founder of a monastic rule either in association with St. Benedict or separately. It has been taken for granted that Chaucer knew what he was talking about, as presumably he did. Yet I can discover elsewhere no hint that the name of St. Maurus was ever connected with the establishment of the Benedictine rule or any other.

The saint was a young disciple of St. Benedict who is known to us only through a brief account by Gregory the Great in the *Dialogues*.[88] It is related that while rescuing a comrade from drowning he walked on the surface of the water. His fame as a holy youth rested on this one passage

85 *CT*, VII,259 and 441.

86 *CT*, III,674.

87 *CT*, I,173.

88 Bk. II,vii.

until the eleventh century. An elaborate life was then composed, attributed by the author to a quite unknown Faustus but certainly written by an abbot of the French monastery of Glanfeuil, a Benedictine house. According to the *vita*, Maurus came to France during the lifetime of St. Benedict and so became the founder of the order in that country. We need not go into the reasons for believing the biography to be a fabrication by Odo of Glanfeuil, since the opinion now held by all competent scholars was reached after long discussion and a close scrutiny of the evidence.[89] According to this legend, the revered abbot of the French monastery was none other than the youth of whom Gregory wrote. We are left with no sure knowledge about the Maurus of Glanfeuil, if indeed he was not altogether the creation of the good Odo, and we do not know just when or how Benedictine houses were first established in France. We do know, however, that St. Gregory's story about Maurus was familiar to Alcuin at Tours towards the end of the eighth century, since with affectionate humor he added the name to that of his young favorite Rabanus.[90]

It should be borne in mind that the *vita* by Pseudo-Faustus gives no hint of any alteration of the Rule by Maurus or of his sharing in the formation of it. Intent as he was on the glorification of the saint, Odo would certainly not have failed to emphasize his hero's influence on the regulations of the order if he had been aware of such an influence. Furthermore, though the history of the Rule has been studied with unusual care, no one has discovered any hint, as far as I know, that St. Maurus helped establish it.[91]

[89] The best brief account of the controversy is perhaps that of D. Schmitz, *Histoire de l'ordre de saint Benoit*, 1942, II,31, note 4.

[90] See F. Kunstmann, *Hrabanus Magnentius Maurus*, 1841, p. 37.

[91] See among recent publications: C. Butler, *Benedictine Monasticism*, 1924; B. Linderbauer, ed., *Regula Monasteriorum*, 1928; J. McCann, *St. Benedict*, 1937; Justo Perez de Urbel, *Historia de la Orden Benedictina*, 1941; D. Schmitz, *op.cit.*; A. Ildefonse Schuster, ed., *S. Benedicti Regula Monasteriorum*, 1945; T. F. Lindsay, *St. Benedict. His Life and Work*,

Yet Chaucer, one must suppose, would not of his own invention have linked Maurus with St. Benedict as he did. There the matter must be left unless or until someone finds new evidence.

Like the allusions to St. Thomas already mentioned, those to other figures from the New Testament and the apocryphal writings developed from it are sometimes confusing. So it is with St. James the Greater and the Less. A sentence from the *Epistle* ascribed to the latter is paraphrased by the Clerk,[92] and the Wife of Bath had made a pilgrimage to the shrine of the former at Compostella.[93] Remembering her pilgrimage and the immense fame of the shrine, we may conclude that she meant James the Greater when she swore "by that lord that called is Seint Jame."[94] On the other hand, the oaths of the eagle in the *House of Fame*,[95] of the Summoner in the *Friar's Tale*,[96] and of Daun John in the *Shipman's Tale*[97] could apply equally well to either saint.

St. Paul is mentioned only once by Chaucer, when his name is coupled with that of St. Peter by the rascally friar of the *Summoner's Tale*, who avers that his study and diligence as a preacher are to speak in "Petres wordes and in Poules."[98] The common feast of the two saints on the 29th of June would have made their juxtaposition as natural to a summoner or a friar as to Chaucer himself. St. Peter's name appears alone not infrequently, half a dozen times in oaths[99] and once in connection with a false

---

1949. The two fifteenth-century translations of the Rule written in northern England do not mention Maurus. Addis and Arnold, *A Catholic Dictionary*, 1884, *sub* Maurists, cites only Chaucer as authority for the statement that Maurus "almost equally with St. Benedict" was responsible for the Rule. The reforming Maurists of the seventeenth century do not concern us.

92 *CT*, IV,1154.
93 *CT*, I,466.
94 *CT*, III,312.
95 *HF*, line 885.
96 *CT*, III,1443.
97 *CT*, VII,355.
98 *CT*, III,1819.
99 *HF*, lines 1034 and 2000; *CT*, III,446,1332, VII,214, VIII,665.

relic among the other absurdities treasured by the Pardoner for business reasons.[100] Perhaps no wholly satisfactory explanation of the reference to St. Peter's sister in the night-spell uttered by the Oxford carpenter in the *Miller's Tale*[101] will ever be found, or for that matter need be sought, since charms like all orally transmitted rhymes are wayward with names. The legend of a daughter, St. Petronilla, was of course generally known. It is a good guess that the sister no less than the brother who is invoked in a charm quoted from *Notes and Queries*[102] by Skeat derives from the story of Petronilla, which in turn is of very uncertain origin. Nothing could better indicate the wild confusion into which the legend drifted than an entry in the martyrology of Sion Monastery which makes Peter's daughter Mary Magdalene.[103] The conflation with the apocryphal history of the apostolate in southern Gaul under the leadership of Maximim and Lazarus is here complete.

Although there are a dozen scattered references to St. John the Evangelist, in all but two the name is used as an oath, including the punning allusion to John of Gaunt at the end of *The Book of the Duchess*:[104]

> A long castel with walles white,
> Be seynt Johan! on a ryche hil.

Otherwise, the strange "feminine creature" of the *House of Fame*[105] had as many eyes as the Four Beasts of the Apocalypse, and the Prioress in exclaiming at the murder of her little hero[106] was reminded of that other passage which describes the song of the virgin host before the celestial Lamb.

The name of St. Anne occurs only once apart from that of the Virgin (as an oath by the profane Summoner of the

[100] *CT*, I,697. [101] *CT*, I,3486. [102] 1 ser., VIII,613.

[103] *The Martiloge*, ed. Dewick and Procter, p. 92.

[104] *BD*, lines 1318-1319. The other nine oaths are found as follows: *PF*, line 451; *Mars*, line 9; *CT*, II,18,1019, III,164,1800,2252, V,596, VI,752.

[105] *HF*, lines 1383-1385. [106] *CT*, VII,580-585.

Friar's Tale)[107] but twice when so coupled. The likelihood that in both instances[108] there is an echo of Dante's *Paradiso,* as suggested in a note by Robinson, appears almost a certainty when one observes that a passage of three stanzas shortly preceding the reference in the prologue to the *Second Nun's Tale* is an evident paraphrase of the opening lines of the canto next following.[109] If this and other such extended passages be counted singly, the name of the Blessed Virgin is introduced nearly twenty-five times, far more frequently, as one would expect, than that of any other saint. Thus, it may be said, is Chaucer's calendar illumined.

There remain half a dozen saints, whose names are casually mentioned or invoked. There is appropriate allusion to the hospitality of St. Julian by the always ready-witted eagle of the *House of Fame,* and the Franklin is termed a regional St. Julian.[110] The two references to St. Giles, both in oaths,[111] have no evident connection with the matters in hand, but bear witness to the extraordinary and unexplained popularity which his cult attained during the eleventh and twelfth centuries both in France and in Great Britain.[112] That the monk of the *Shipman's Tale* should swear in swift succession by St. Martin and St. Denis[113] is not inappropriate, since the scene of the story is the prosperous town dedicated to the latter. Neither saint is elsewhere mentioned. The single reference to St. Simon is in an oath by the sick man in the *Summoner's Tale.*[114] It so happens that one of the friars in the fabliau by Jean de Bai-

[107] *CT,* III,1613.
[108] *CT,* II,641-642, VIII,69-70.
[109] See Bryan and Dempster, *Sources and Analogues,* pp. 664-665.
[110] *HF,* line 1022; *CT,* I,340.
[111] *HF,* line 1183; *CT,* VIII,1185.
[112] The statement that St. Giles, being lame, became the patron of cripples, and so of beggars, and so of travellers, who were therefore provided with churches outside the gates of towns in which to hear mass while their horses were being shod, appears to be a finespun fancy. Lydgate in his poem on the saint calls him "of poore folk cheef patroun."
[113] *CT,* VII,148,151.
[114] *CT,* III,2094.

sieux, which is the closest analogue of Chaucer's tale yet discovered, is named Simon, but the correspondence is more curious than important. Another casual reference is that of the angry Host at the conclusion of the *Pardoner's Tale*,[115] who swears "by the croys which that Seint Eleyne fond," which is the sole allusion to the legend of the invention of the True Cross.

Finally, there is the invocation of St. Judocus by the Wife of Bath:[116]

> But he was quit, by God and by Seint Joce!
> I made hym of the same wode a croce.

It is difficult to see why the name of this seventh-century hermit was introduced, unless indeed Skeat's conjecture is correct that a quatrain from Jean de Meun's *Testament* came to Chaucer's mind while composing the Wife of Bath's argumentative apology. She is recounting at the moment how she got the better of her fourth husband, the *revelour*, repaying him for his infidelities. In the *Testament*, which is a wise and witty poem too much neglected, the misbehavior of husbands is under review at the point with which we are concerned.[117]

> Quant dame Katherine voit l'espreuve dant Joce
> Qui por l'amour sa fame ne donne une beloce,
> Si dobte que li sien ne li face autel noce,
> Si li refait sovent d'autel fut une croce.

Skeat's comment on the fourth line of the quatrain is too complacent: "It is obvious that Chaucer has copied this in l. 484, and that he has here found his rime to *croce*." To which it may be replied that Chaucer—most adept of craftsmen—surely never needed to go hunting for a rhyme. It must be observed, too, that "dant Joce" is far from being

[115] *CT*, VI,951.
[116] *CT*, III,483-484.
[117] *Roman de la Rose*, ed. M. Méon, 1814, IV,24, lines 461-464.

a saint. Jean's quatrain did not supply the name of St. Judocus. Yet I believe that Skeat was right in thinking that the quatrain suggested the form of the couplet, probably without any consciousness of the transaction on Chaucer's part. The situation is the same. A wife is repaying a husband for injuries received—"d'autel fut une croce," "of the same wode a croce." So the Wife of Bath might well express herself in a phrase echoed from a poem which Chaucer knew well.

And St. Joce for "dant Joce"? Judocus was far from being a saint well known in England, and even in France he was not widely renowned. No English church was dedicated to him, though across the Channel in Picardy his cult was preserved through a monastery founded on the site of his hermitage. Chaucer may very well have known this establishment, which was on the coast near Étaples. It is worth noting, furthermore, that he appears in the Westminster calendar, sharing December 13 with St. Lucy. As we have seen, all but seven of the saints to whom Chaucer referred are found in that list. It is reasonable to suppose that he would have learned the odd name of the saint either from a service-book or from experience as a traveller. While composing the Wife of Bath's speech, he might well, we may further surmise, recall the name at the very moment the quatrain from the *Testament* stirred in his memory. It is useless to speculate whether "dant Joce" suggested "Seint Joce" or "Seint Joce" "dant Joce." At all events, the relationship of the couplet to the quatrain illustrates in a small but neat way one of the processes of poetic creation.

Such a survey as we have been making of Chaucer's allusions to saints and their legends is variously revealing. Their frequency and range are accepted by the reader of our time as being completely natural, though we are well aware that in an author of later date they would seem an affectation. In this respect as in so many others Chaucer was altogether of his own age, reporting not only what he heard but what he felt in common with most other men of the same background and station. Yet there is more in it than that. He was steeped in the lore of the Church but not equally, we must observe, in all aspects of it. He was a lettered man, a man who had read widely, considering the activities of his life, but he was not a scholar in the sense that he set himself to the solution of problems for himself. His acquirements were made without much conscious effort, we may believe, and they were about matters for which he had a native aptitude. Not a philosopher, not a theologian, he accepted ideas rather than generated them. Yet he was a man of very profound wisdom in the ways of the human mind and heart.

To him the legends of the Church would inevitably have furnished a fascinating panorama. He would have remembered what he read or heard because what he so learned gave him something on which his imagination throve. As I have already pointed out, he did not often quote the words of saints themselves, and only in the *Second Nun's Tale* did he make a legend the theme of a poem, but the allusions are thickly sown. They are an essential element in his work, as the lore of saints was in his life, and they cannot be either neglected or despised by anyone who wishes to know him as he was.

ii · the social status of the franklin

An uncertainty as to the social position of franklins in general, and of Chaucer's Franklin in particular, has occasionally manifested itself since the early part of the nineteenth century. In 1810, Todd[1] quoted an elaborate note from Waterhous's *Commentary* on Sir John Fortescue's *De Laudibus Legum Angliae,* which tended to show that franklins did not belong to the gentry. Todd was unable to square this with the fact that Chaucer's Franklin was "at sessiouns," since by a statute of Edward III,[2] which he cited, justices were *seigneurs,* and that he was "ofte tyme" a knight of the shire, since by another statute[3] members of parliament were "chivalers et serjantz des meulz vaues du paies." Todd was thus left in doubt as to the gentility of the Franklin. As a later examination of Fortescue's remarks will show, it is not he but his commentator who must be blamed for lowering the status of Chaucer's sanguine country gentleman. If Todd had been of firmer mind, or if he had studied the subject more deeply, he would not have left the matter in doubt—a trap for unwary feet in later times.

One cannot be sure that Henry Bradley consulted Todd before passing the definition of "franklin" in *N.E.D.,* but he may have been influenced by it. In any case, the examples quoted in the article certainly do not warrant of themselves the flat-footed statement as printed:

> 2. A freeholder; in 14-15th c. the designation of a class of landowners, of free but not noble birth, and ranking next below the gentry.

[1] H. J. Todd, *Illustrations of the Lives and Writings of Gower and Chaucer,* pp. 247-249.

[2] 34 Edw. III, cap. 1.

[3] 46 Edw. III.

The first clause is, of course, indisputable, since nobody has ever ranked franklins among the nobility. The last clause, however, is open to serious challenge.

The matter would perhaps have remained one of legal and lexicographical interest only, if in 1906 Root had not accepted Bradley's definition without question and based upon it an interpretation of Chaucer's Franklin that was novel and ingenious rather than sound—as I shall endeavor to show.

> The Franklin [he wrote] has much in common with the better type of the "self-made man." He has at his disposal all that money can buy, and he has held office in his own county; but he is uncomfortably conscious of a certain lack of "gentility,"—betrayed by his fondness for the words "gentil" and "gentilesse,"—and of the full education which would adorn his prosperous estate. . . . Conscious that, with all that he has acquired and attained, he can never be quite the complete gentleman, he would fain be the father of a gentleman; but his hopes are disappointed by the unfortunate vulgar proclivities of his son and heir.[4]

The Franklin is, in short, a parvenu. If Root had not had in mind the clause for which Bradley stands responsible, "ranking next below the gentry," it is unlikely that he would have felt any lack in the rather learned and eminently dignified figure whom Chaucer drew. He might have asked himself how the Franklin acquired his property and rose in the world, about which there is no hint; and he might have remembered squires' sons and baronets' sons, and even scions of the peerage, who in English novels and plays of later time have shown a taste for the company of their social inferiors, as well as a deplorable tendency "to

[4] R. K. Root, *The Poetry of Chaucer*, 1906 (rev. edn. 1922), pp. 271-272.

pleye at dees, and to despende"—or to commit the equivalent follies of their age.

It shows the influence of Professor Root's admirable book that Professor Kittredge, in another admirable book, should have betrayed by a casual sentence his acceptance of the view just quoted. "The Franklin," he remarks, "is a wealthy man, ambitious to found a family."[5] The statement is in no way elaborated or defended, which has its significance. In less than a dozen years, it seems, an ill-supported interpretation had acquired such legendary value that it could be stated with dogmatic precision.

Yet this reading of Chaucer's lines is quite unwarranted by the evidence I have been able to gather. Warton was certainly right when he said of the Franklin that he was "a country gentleman," although the second part of the definition he gave, "whose estate consisted in free land,"[6] could be more accurately put.

Let us see, to begin with, what clues Chaucer actually gives us as to the social status of his Franklin. (1) He was in the company of a "Sergeant of the Lawe."[7] (2) He was wealthy and lived generously on his land.[8] (3) He was "lord and sire" at "sessiouns,"[9] which means that he sat importantly as justice in petty sessions. (4) He had often been "knight of the shire," representing his county in parliament.[10] (5) He had been a sheriff.[11] (6) He had been a "countour," probably auditing the accounts of the sheriff.[12] (7) He was a "vavasour"—none "worthier."[13] He calls himself a "burel man" and says that he never slept on Parnassus, learned Cicero, or acquainted himself with the colors of rhetoric,[14] which are certainly the half-humorous deprecations of a person who made no pretence of clerkly

[5] G. L. Kittredge, *Chaucer and His Poetry*, 1915, p. 204.
[6] *History of English Poetry*, edn. 1840, II,202.
[7] *CT*, I,331. [8] *CT*, I,335-354. [9] *CT*, I,355.
[10] *CT*, I,356. [11] *CT*, I,359. [12] *loc.cit.*
[13] *CT*, I,360. [14] *CT*, V,716-726.

lore, though he showed sufficient learning in his tale. Each of these points has significance, and, taken together, they offer very complete and interesting confirmation of the Franklin's position as a member of the landed gentry. Before considering them, however, we had best see whether, by examining the evidence, we cannot reach a clearer notion of what the term "franklin" really means than is afforded by the dictionaries.

In a couple of cases that have been recorded the word certainly indicates a freeman as distinguished from a villein, without further suggestion of rank. About 1440 it was glossed "libertinus" in the *Promptuarium Parvulorum*, which is uncompromising enough. Similarly in a *Vita Haroldi*, written about 1300, we read that the wounded king was carried off the battlefield "a duobus ut fertur mediocribus viris quos francalanos sive agricolas vocant agnitus."[15] There can be no doubt, I think, that the unknown author regarded franklins as very low creatures indeed. Mätzner in his *Sprachproben* and the editors of *N.E.D.* were probably justified, with the support of these two instances, in giving "freeman" as one meaning of "franklin," but scarcely in supposing it to be the primary one.

All the other illustrations that I have been able to find—and considerable searching has not enabled me to add notably to the collections previously made—refer to the franklin as a member of a landholding class, and, when scrutinized closely, to a class of very good social position. At least, the context makes this so abundantly clear in most instances that one can no longer doubt the propriety of calling the franklin a gentleman. Even in the thirteenth century, I make out, he was the equivalent of the country squire of modern England.

The three earliest examples of the word that have been found are in charters. The first of these is from 1166, dur-

[15] Ed. W. deG. Birch, 1885, p. 34.

ing the reign of Henry II. In a grant to Cernel Abbey, we read: "Super dominium ecclesiae sunt feoda trium militum et dimidii, cum tenura Francolensium in villa Cernae. Quisque autem istorum debet facere wardam ad praeceptum vestrum apud Castellum de Corfe uno mense per annum."[16] The number of franklins is not mentioned, but they must have been men of some importance if they severally had the duty of guarding Corfe Castle. Their wealth would depend upon their number, the aggregate of their holdings being to the amount of three and a half knights' fees, unless—as is possible—they had holdings from other overlords than the abbey. At all events, these franklins must have been persons of substance and consideration.

The next two examples are in *Charter Rolls* from the reign of John, and both from charters given to conventual establishments. The first specifies as one of the holdings of a convent "unam carrucatam terrae apud Hamerwich cum villanis et franchelano."[17] The second reads: "confirmamus omnia feuda militum et franccolanorum qui tenent de eodem monasterio et quod habeant octo hundreda sua et justiciam de eisdem hundredis libere et quiete et plenarie cum omnibus libertatibus."[18] In the first of these cases, which is specific, the franklin could not have been a very wealthy person, since an estate of between 160 and 180 acres would hardly put him out of the company of "dirt farmers"—to use an admirable Americanism. At the same time, he would have the villeins as laborers, and he may have done very well. In the second case, it will be noted that knights and franklins are mentioned in the same phrase as holding from the monastery, and apparently on the same

[16] *Red Book of the Exchequer*, ed. H. Hall, 1896 (Rolls Ser. 99), 1,212. Quoted in DuCange from the *Liber niger Scaecarii*, concerning which see Hall's introduction.

[17] *Rotuli Chartarum*, ed. T. D. Hardy, Record Com., 1837, p. 43, col. 1.

[18] *ibid.*, p. 82, col. 1.

terms. The only distinction between them which appears is one of titular rank, rather than of tenure.

It is an interesting fact that as early as the thirteenth century Le Fraunkeleyn was used as a surname, and for persons who, if inheritances and holdings of land may be taken to indicate anything, had a very solid—if not brilliant—social position.[19] As a matter of fact, we could scarcely have better evidence than this of the assured position of the class.

We may next examine a group of references by versifiers who wrote at the end of the thirteenth century or in the fourteenth. The first of them is the shadowy Robert of Gloucester, who in his account of King Lear thus warned parents against giving up their land to their children:

Vor wel may a simple frankelein . in miseise him so bringe.
Of lute lond wanne þer biuel . such cas of an kinge.[20]

"Simple franklin" he is called, but, please note, in contrast to royal majesty: quite as if one should set off a member of the squirearchy against the king.

An example from *Cursor Mundi* is instructive in another way. The author is reporting the conversation of Jacob with Pharaoh, who says of the magnificent Joseph:

First he was here als our thain
But now es he for ai franckelain.[21]

Considering the honors held by Joseph at the time, it would seem that Pharaoh was meant to imply more by his antithesis than the mere contrast of freedom with serfdom. One

19 See, for example, the *Calendar of Patent Rolls* and *Calendar of Close Rolls*, as well as the *Excerpta e Rotulis Finium in Turri Londinensi*, ed. C. Roberts, 1836, which cover the years 1216-1272. The use of settled surnames for people above the lower classes is a phenomenon of earlier date than is sometimes supposed.

20 *Metrical Chronicle*, ed. W. A. Wright, 1887 (Rolls Ser. 86), 1,61, lines 821-822. Dated 1290-1300.

21 *Cursor Mundi*, dated 1300-1325, ed. R. Morris, 1874-1893 (EETS), lines 5373-5374.

must not press this too hard, to be sure, since the author needed a rhyme. The couplet could never have been written, however, if early in the fourteenth century franklins were considered to belong to the lower orders.

Nor, surely, would Nicolas Trivet have set down in his Anglo-Norman *Chroniques* that "Thomas Brotherton (filius R. Edouardi I) apres le mort son pere esposa la fille de un Frauncelein appelle Alice."[22] It makes little difference that modern historians aver that the Earl of Norfolk's father-in-law was Sir Thomas Hales of Harwich, or that Trivet's statement is manifestly absurd in one particular, since Thomas of Brotherton was not born until 1300, while his father died in 1307. The point is that a contemporary chronicler could confuse a knight with a franklin after this fashion. Evidently he recognized no wide gulf between the two classes.

Of two examples of the word from Robert Mannyng of Brunne, one is amusing rather than important, though it couples franklins with squires, which—as we shall soon see —was an exact equation in the fifteenth century, at least. Conan sends to Dianot for his daughter Ursula,

> And gentil damysels vngyuen,
> Þat able to mennes companye were þryuen,—
> Squyers doughtres, & frankelayns,
> To gyue hem to knyghtes & to swayns.[23]

The difficulty here is to find the meaning that Robert can have attached to "swayns." His second example is more useful to us. In regard to the Statute of Mortmain, in the second part of his *Chronicle,* he wrote:

[22] Unfortunately I have to quote this from Spelman, *Glossarium Archaiologicum,* 1664, *sub* "Francling," since the chronicle has not yet been edited. It is said to have been written about 1334, which was four years before the death of Thomas.

[23] *The Story of England,* ed. F. J. Furnivall, 1887 (Rolls Ser. 87), I,230, lines 6545-6548. Dated 1338.

Was mad an oþer statut, þat non erle no baroun,
No oþer lorde stoute, ne fraunkeleyn of toun,
Tille holy kirke salle gyue tenenement, rent no lond.[24]

The corresponding lines in Pierre de Langtoft's *Chronicle*, which was Robert's source, run as follows:

Est fet l'estatut, ke counte, ne baroun,
Ne seygnur de terre, parmi la regioun,
Face à seinte Eglise offrand ne doun
De terre ne tenement, si par cungé noun
Du rays e de son consayl.[25]

Robert apparently felt that "lorde stoute" was not a sufficient translation for "seygnur de terre" and so added "fraunkeleyn of toun."[26]

In *Piers Plowman* we find "franklin" used three times. In the first instance, the Dreamer in the guise of an idle London priest is conversing with Reason. In an obviously ironic strain he talks about the privileges of the clergy, chief among them being idleness. He then says:

For shold no clerk be crouned . bote yf he ycome were
Of franklens and free men . and of folke yweddede.
Bondmen and bastardes . and beggers children,
Thuse by-longeth to labour . and lordes kyn to seruen
Bothe god and good men . as here degree asketh.[27]

There is a contrast here between bond and free, it is true; but the whole implication of the passage is that franklins

[24] Ed. as by Pierre de Langtoft by T. Hearne, 1725, p. 239. This part of Robert's work is not in Furnivall's edition. It was based on Pierre de Langtoft, which explains Hearne's error of ascription.

[25] Ed. T. Wright. 1866-1868 (Rolls Ser. 47), II,174.

[26] This phrase is illustrated by a writ analyzed in *Calendar of Inquisitions Miscellaneous*, ed. H. C. Maxwell Lyte, 1916, II,56, no. 233. In this writ, dated 1 Sept. 9 Edward II (1315), Thomas de Polington is described as "lord of the whole town of Polington." "Town" was doubtless used in the sense familiar to all New Englanders.

[27] Ed. W. W. Skeat, 1886, C, Pass. vi, 63-67.

are gentlefolk. From the second instance in *Piers Plowman* no satisfactory conclusions can be drawn, I think; but it should be noted in passing. Wit is discoursing about the contrariety of "Westminster law," in that it visits the sins of the fathers upon the children.

> For thauh the fader be a frankelayne . and for a felon
> be hanged,
> The heritage that the air sholde haue . ys at the kynges
> wille.[28]

It is hard to tell whether the franklin is here taken as an example of high degree or low. The third case is, however, quite conclusive as to the writer's estimate of the social position of franklins. Conscience is the speaker. Jesus, he says, was knight, king, and conqueror, having by virtue of conquest the right:

> To make lordes of laddes . of londe that he wynneth
> And fre men foule thralles . that folweth nouȝt his lawes.
> The Iuwes, that were gentil-men . Iesu thei dispised,
> Bothe his lore and his lawe . now ar thei lowe cherlis.
> As wyde as the worlde is . wonyeth there none
> But vnder tribut and taillage . as tykes and cherles.
> And tho that bicome Crysten . by conseille of the baptiste,
> Aren frankeleynes, fre men . thorw fullyng that thei toke,
> And gentel-men with Iesu . for Iesus was yfulled,
> And vppon Caluarye on crosse . ycrouned kynge of
> Iewes.[29]

In the opinion of the B redactor of Piers Plowman, which the C redactor saw no reason to dispute, franklins were not only freemen, but they were gentlemen. This one passage would be sufficient of itself to refute the notion that they ranked "next below the gentry." It shows the fallibility of

[28] C, Pass. xi, 240-241.

[29] B, Pass. xix, 32-41. In C, Pass. xxii, 32-41.

any system whatsoever that this quotation actually appears in *N.E.D.*, but without the fine and significant phrase "gentelmen with Iesu," and is used to illustrate the meaning "freeman."

From the first half of the fifteenth century we have detailed and precise evidence of another kind as to the position of franklins. It comes from a source that could not be bettered—a book of etiquette. In the nature of things, the John Russell who compiled this *Book of Nurture* had to put his mind on questions of precedence. He gives [30] as the estates "equal with a knight," who sit at table three or four to a mess, the following: abbot and prior "sans mitre," dean, arch-deacon, Master of Rolls, under justices, barons of the King's Exchequer, provincial of a religious order, doctor of divinity, doctor of "both laws," prothonotary, pope's collector, and mayor of the staple. At a squire's table, sitting four to a mess, come sergeants of law, late mayors of London, masters of chancery, all "prechers, residencers, and persones that ar greable," apprentices of law, merchants, and franklins. This list seems to us, perhaps, slightly whimsical, but it could doubtless have been defended in each particular by John Russell. Incidentally it gives evidence as to the social esteem into which merchants had come by the fourteenth and fifteenth centuries, when their position was certainly higher than in later times. They ranked with the gentry. That all the folk mentioned in the second list were so regarded is made clear by still another list of those who eat with squires,[31] which does not mention franklins but which ends with "gentlemen and gentlewomen." The whole matter was evidently quite clear in John Russell's mind.

We may now return to Sir John Fortescue, who was men-

30 *The Babees Book*, ed. F. J. Furnivall, 1868 (EETS 32), pp. 188-189.
31 *ibid.*, p. 187.

tioned earlier. In his famous *De Laudibus Legum Angliae*, which was composed between 1468 and 1471, he wrote:

> Regio eciam illa ita respersa refertaque est possessoribus terrarum et agrorum, quod in ea villula tam parva reperiri non poterit in qua non est miles, armiger, vel paterfamilias qualis ibidem frankeleyn vulgariter nuncupatur. magnis ditatus possessionibus; necnon libere tenentes alii, et valetti plurimi suis patrimoniis sufficientes ad faciendum juratum in forma prenotata.[32]

In the excellent translation of 1775, reprinted in Amos' edition, this runs:

> England is so thick-spread and filled with rich and landed men, that there is scarce a small village in which you may not find a knight, an esquire, or some substantial householder, commonly called, a Frankleyne; all men of considerable estates: there are others who are called Freeholders, and many Yeomen of estates sufficient to make a substantial Jury, within the description before observed.[33]

As Fortescue goes on to comment on the wealth of some of the "valetti" and as he clearly classifies the franklins with the knights and esquires rather than with the "libere tenentes alii," we may conclude that his notions coincided with those of John Russell. Franklins were gentlefolk.

Chaucer's Franklin, however, was not simply a member of a large and flourishing class: he had individual characteristics and distinctions, which throw light on the possibilities open to men of his rank and serve at the same time to fix his personal status. I have enumerated above eight such points. Most of them are worthy of brief notice, and some of them deserve close study.

[32] Cap. 29. Ed. S. B. Chrimes, 1942, p. 68.
[33] Ed. A. Amos, 1825, p. 104.

The Franklin was, in the first place, going to Canterbury in the company of a Sergeant of the Law, whose learning and success are equally emphasized. The association was a natural one. Not only were the two men of the same rank, as we have seen to be the case on the testimony of John Russell, given above; but they would have had associations in public and private business that might have led to friendship. The Man of Law, it will be remembered, had often sat as justice of assizes, "by patente, and by plein commissioun,"[34] where the Franklin would have been in attendance both as an important landholder and as a "countour," not to mention the litigation in which men of any substance seem almost continuously to have been engaged during the fourteenth and fifteenth centuries. Although Chaucer cannot have been using "countour" in quite the sense in which it was taken by John Selden in his *Titles of Honour,* when he wrote: "For a *countour* was, if I am not deceived, a serjeant at law, known also then by both names,"[35] it is clear that the Franklin not only understood business but had also some knowledge of the law. In this connection, it may be observed that "sergeant" seems to have been used not only of lawyers but to designate propertied gentlemen who were not knights. In a statute of Edward III[36] we read that neither men of law "pursuant busoignes en la Court le Roi," nor sheriffs during their terms of office, shall be returned to parliament as knights of shires. "Mes voet le Roi, que Chivalers et serjantz des meulz vaues du paies soient retornez." Of similar import is a reference in Pierre de Langtoft's *Chronicle.* The members of a military expedition to Gascony are thus designated:

[34] The meaning of these terms is well illustrated by a reference to sheriffs in *Statutes of the Realm,* 28 Edw. III, cap. 9 (1354): "viscontes de diverses contees, par vertue des commissions et briefs generals."

[35] *Works,* 1726, III,1027. Selden quotes the *Mirror of Justices* ("Chez le seigneur Coke en l'epist. du 9. livre"): "Countors sont serjeants, sachans la ley del royalm."

[36] *Statutes of the Realm,* 46 Edw. III (1372).

> Barouns e vavasours de gentil lynage,
> Chuvalers et serjauns of lur cosinage,
> Gens à pé sanz noumbre de more et boscage.[37]

These sergeants may safely be equated with franklins.

That the wealth of Chaucer's Franklin was not exceptional we know from the testimony of Sir John Fortescue, already quoted. He was no upstart, but like a vast number of other untitled gentlemen of the time had great possessions. The notion that peers and knights were the only important landlords in the complicated world of feudal tenure is a serious mistake, though perhaps a natural one. In reading the *Calendars of Inquisitions* for the reigns of Edward III and Richard II, one is impressed by the size of the holdings of men who were neither noblemen nor knights. Some of these wealthy commoners had land scattered over several counties.[38] The Inquisitions prove very conclusively both the wealth and the importance of men below the estate of knights. In the light of all this, it seems in no way odd that Chaucer's Friar, who must have loved good cheer, should have made himself beloved and familiar.

> With frankeleyns over al in his contree.[39]

Nor was it strange that Chaucer should have stressed the food and drink in his Franklin's house. John Russell's *Book of Nurture* may again serve to illustrate the point. Russell gives a rhymed bill of fare, headed "A fest for a franklen,"[40] which would have been adequate, one would think, for any earl or baron. In the fifteenth century, as well as in the fourteenth, the landed gentry seem to have been fairly prosperous.

37 Langtoft's *Chronicle,* ed. T. Wright, 1866-1868 (Rolls Ser. 47), II,230.

38 See the case of John Giffard: VII, nos. 78, 180; IX, no. 686. This same Giffard may possibly be referred to elsewhere without specific designation.

39 *CT,* I,216.

40 See Furnivall, *The Babees Book,* pp. 170-171.

There is every justification, indeed, for the following remarks of Thomas Fuller:

> And here under favour I conceive, that if a strict inquiry should be made after the ancient gentry of England, most of them would be found amongst such middle-sized persons as are above two hundred, and beneath a thousand pounds of annual revenue. . . . Men of great estates, in national broils, have smarted deeply for their visible engagements, to the ruin of their families, whereof we have too many sad experiments, whilst such persons who are moderately mounted above the level of common people into a competency, above want and beneath envy, have, by God's blessing on their frugality, continued longest in their conditions, entertaining all alterations in the state with the less destructive change unto themselves.[41]

In a word, the country gentleman, well-to-do or passably rich, flourished in the fourteenth century quite as much as in the seventeenth century, or in the nineteenth.

Such men, naturally enough, were not infrequently chosen to represent their counties in parliament. A scrutiny of the lists of persons summoned during the reigns of Edward III, Richard II, and Henry IV shows that a knight of the shire was by no means always a knight in degree, although it is true that he commonly held that rank. Unless a gentleman was by birth and estate an outstanding figure, it is evident, he would scarcely have been returned. Certain counties were more prone than others to elect untitled men, but the honor was largely reserved for knights. It is all the more notable that Chaucer's Franklin had been in parliament "ful ofte tyme." Like everything else that is said of him, this shows that he was an eminent man in his shire. And of course he was a gentleman by token of his

[41] *Worthies of England* (1662), ed. P. A. Nuttall, 1840, I,63.

election, for it would have been contrary to law as well as of custom to send a lesser person to Westminster. A statute of 1372, already quoted, says specifically: "Mes voet le Roi, que Chivalers et serjantz des meulz vaues du paies soient retornez."[42] Even more explicit is a law of the following century, which provides that knights of shires

> soient notablez Chivalers des mesmez lez Counteez pour lez queux ils serront issint esluz, ou autrement tielx notablez Esquiers gentils homez del Nativite dez mesmez les Counteez comme soient ablez destre Chivalers, & null home destre tiel Chivaler que estoise en la degree de vadlet & desouth.[43]

That Chaucer's Franklin had been a sheriff indicates quite as clearly as his return to parliament that he was a man of high position in his county. "For," as Thomas Fuller rightly says, "the principal gentry in every shire, of most ancient extractions and best estates, were deputed for that place."[44] Indeed, the post of viscount, or sheriff, was a great honor in medieval England, although in duties and in expense it made a heavy tax on its occupant. Any examination of documents issuing from the court, like the Close Rolls or the Parliamentary Writs, shows the importance and the extraordinary variety of the business that fell to the lot of the king's local representative. Men of standing were chosen for the office, since no one who lacked either social prestige or personal ability could possibly have succeeded in it. A very good understanding of the place held by the sheriff can be obtained by reading the great legal treatise of the mid-thirteenth century, Henry de Bracton's *De Legibus et Consuetudinibus Angliae.*[45] No one who has perused Bracton will be in danger of underestimating the position of sheriff in the medieval English system.

[42] *Statutes of the Realm,* 46 Edw. III.

[43] *ibid.,* 23 Hen. VI, cap. 14.

[44] *Worthies of England,* I,61.

[45] Ed. G. E. Woodbine, 1922; or T. Twiss, 1878 (Rolls Ser. 70).

The care with which sheriffs were selected is well shown by Sir John Fortescue, to whose witness I have already appealed. He says that on the morrow of All Souls a large group of specified high officers of the Crown meet in the Court of Exchequer,

> ubi hii omnes communi assensu nominant de quolibet comitatu tres milites vel armigeros, quos inter ceteros ejusdem comitatus ipsi opinantur melioris esse deposicionis et fame, et ad officium vicecomitis illius melius dispositos, ex quibus rex unum tantum eligit.[46]

It would be beside the point to inquire whether the sheriffs so selected invariably used their power to the common advantage of all. Our present interest is not in the history of the sheriff's office—which would be a fascinating study —but only in its high esteem during the Middle Ages.

Chaucer says, finally, of his Franklin that nowhere was there "such a worthy vavasour." In regard to this I have met with no comment so good as that of the learned John Selden, from whose observations it will be useful to quote the most pertinent sections. "The use and continuance of the name of vavasor was such, that from the Normans, until the time of Henry IV, it was a name known; but feudal only, not at all honorary."[47] "And the author of *Fleta* (lib. i, cap 5, §4): sub regibus sunt comites & barones, duces, milites, magnates, vavasores, & alii subditi ut liberi & servi, qui omnes aetatem xii annorum ad minus habentes ferre tenentur regi fidelitatis sacramentum."[48] "Now for the nature of a vavasour; though we perhaps may soon miss in giving an exact definition of him, yet it is plain that he was ever beneath a baron. And it seems he was in the more antient times only a tenant by knight's service, that either

[46] *op.cit.*, p. 54, cap. 24.

[47] *Titles of Honour, Works,* 1726, III,660.

[48] *ibid.*, III,661. See *Fleta, seu Commentarius Juris Anglicani,* 1685, p. 2.

held of a mesne lord, and not immediately of the king, or at least of the king as of an honour or mannor, and not in chief, both of which excluded him from the dignity of a baron by tenure."[49] Very justly Selden says of Chaucer's calling the Franklin a vavasour: "It is likely that he gave him this title, as the best, and above what he had before commended him for. Neither would he have put it as an addition of worth to a *sheriff* and a *countour*, unless it had been of special note and honour."[50]

John Selden's wisdom is shown not least of all in his conclusion that "we perhaps may soon miss in giving an exact definition" of a vavasour. Modern historians have been equally at a loss to define the term with precision. F. W. Maitland said of it: "Whatever else we may think of these vavassores, they are not barons and probably they are not immediate tenants of the king."[51] In Pollock and Maitland's *History of English Law* there occurs this further unsatisfactory statement: "Neither the theory that the *vavassor* must needs be a vassal's vassal, nor the derivation of his name from *vassi vassorum* can be regarded as certain. In England the word is rare."[52]

Comparatively rare, no doubt, it is; yet it was recognized, and was perhaps no more indefinite in meaning on English than on French soil, where the term appears to have been used with considerable latitude. Henry de Bracton, who has been cited above in reference to sheriffs, was certainly not in doubt as to the position of vavasours in the thirteenth century, although his description of them leaves something still to be desired.

> Item in temporalibus imperatores, reges, et principes in his quae pertinent ad regnum, et sub eis duces, comites

49 *loc.cit.*
50 *ibid.*, III,1027 (note no. 248, to fol. 661).
51 *Domesday Book and Beyond*, 1897, p. 87.
52 2nd edn. 1899, I,546, note 1.

> et barones, magnates sive vavasores, et milites, et etiam liberi et villani, et diversae potestates sub rege constitutae. . . . Sunt et alii potentes sub rege, qui barones dicuntur, hoc est robur belli. Sunt etiam alii qui dicuntur vavasores, viri magnae dignitatis. Vavasor enim nihil melius dici poterit quam vas sortitum ad valetudinem. Sunt etiam sub rege milites, scilicet ad militiam exercendam electi, et cum rege et supradictis militent.[53]

It is interesting to notice that Bracton mentions vavasours after barons but before knights, and implies a distinction of kind, as if barons and vavasours represented social grades, while knights were functionaries in the business of war. There is no doubt, it seems to me, that the vavasour, like the baron, was thought of in connection with his feudal tenure of land rather than in his military capacity, although he owed service to his lord as much as any knight. He was a smaller man than a baron, but a man of the same sort. This is substantiated by another remark of Bracton's, when he is discussing rights of dower: "Sed quod dicitur de baronia non est observandum in vavassoria vel aliis minoribus foedis quam baronia, quia caput non habent sicut baronia."[54] Knighthood was in another category. To Bracton, apparently, the two estates were not commensurable; and if so to him in the thirteenth century, it would be idle for us in the twentieth to attempt to establish the precise social value of each. What is pertinent to our present inquiry is this: on Bracton's evidence, the vavasour was a landholder of considerable importance. Bracton says nothing about the nature of his tenure, which perhaps means that the distinction between tenants-in-chief and sub-tenants appeared less sharp to the medieval lawyer than to

[53] *De Legibus et Consuetudinibus Angliae,* ed. Woodbine, p. 23; Twiss, I,36-38.

[54] Woodbine, p. 269; Twiss, II,60.

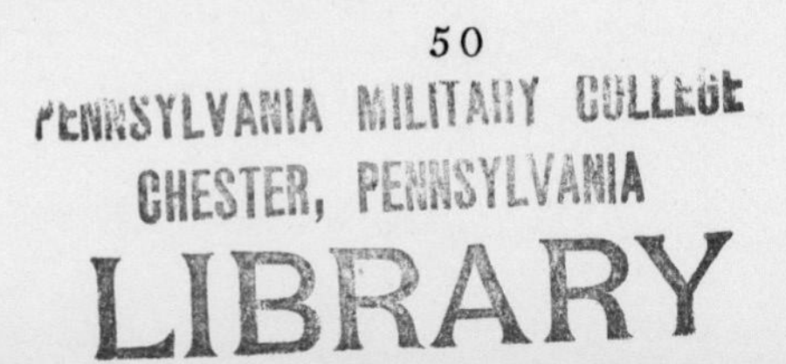

the modern historian. At all events, the vavasour was a magnate, and a person of dignity.

This is borne out by the use of the term by other writers than Chaucer. Pierre de Langtoft, who died about 1307, employed it three times in his *Chronicle.* In the first instance, which has already been quoted to illustrate the use of "sergeant," he was describing a body of troops, among whom he mentioned:

> Barouns e vavasours de gentil lynage
> Chuvalers et serjauns of lur cosinage,
> Gens à pé sanz noumbre de more et boscage.[55]

In the second case, a military force was again in question. King Edward sent to relieve Dunbar:

> Le counte de Garenne, of tut son poer,
> Le counte de Warwyk, et Huge le Despenser;
> Barouns et vavassours, chuvaler, esquyer,
> Surays et Norays, i alaynt de bon quer.[56]

The third quotation is self-explanatory:

> A cele mesavenue estaient tuez
> Vavassours curtoys de gentil parentez.[57]

It is evident that Pierre de Langtoft regarded vavasours as gentlefolk, and as only a little lower than barons.

Only a few decades later, Robert Mannyng of Brunne used the word in describing King Arthur's allocation of lands after his conquests on the Continent:

> He gaf also sire Beduer,
> Þat was of fe his boteler,
> He gaf hym in fe all Normandie,
> But þenne hit was cald Neustrie,
> Boloyne he gaf to sire Holdyn,

[55] *op.cit.*, II,230. [56] *ibid.*, II,240. [57] *ibid.*, II,298.

And Mayne to Borel his cosyn;
He gaf giftes of honurs,
& landes & rentes, to vauasours.[58]

In this passage the term is comparatively colorless, but it in no way contradicts the usage of Langtoft.

A line from the English *Sir Ferumbras,* which was written in Chaucer's time, appears at first sight to offer a contradiction. It runs:

Litel prowesse for me it were wiþ a vauasour for to melle.[59]

The implication that a vavasour was a person of low estate is, however, seen to be false when the context is considered. Ferumbras is talking foolishly at the moment to none other than the great Oliver. A braggart, he would have it understood that dukes and earls are the only proper antagonists for so great a warrior. There is nothing here to upset the notion elsewhere obtained that a vavasour was a person of social distinction.

It is perhaps worth while, in concluding our study of the word, to quote the opinion of Camden, who gives an account of the social orders in England as a part of the introduction to his *Britain.* He is more fantastic than John Selden, but he deserves attention.

> *Vavasores,* sive *Valvasores,* proximum post Barones locum olim tenuerunt, quos à Valvis Iuridici deducunt. Franci, cum in Italia rerum potirentur, *Valvasores* illos dixerunt, qui à Duce, Marchione, Comite, aut Capitaneo plebem, plebisve partem acceperant. Rara haec fuit apud nos dignitas, & siqua fuit, jam paulatim desiit. Nobiles minores sunt Equites aurati, Armigeri, qui vulgo Generosi, et Gentlemen dicuntur.[60]

58 *The Story of England,* ed. Furnivall, p. 384.
59 Ed. S. J. Herrtage, 1879 (EETS 34), p. 16.
60 William Camden, *Britannia,* 1617, p. 86.

Later he remarks:

> Generosi vel promiscue nobiles sunt, qui natalibus clari, aut quos virtus aut fortuna e faece hominum extulit.[61]

It must have struck the reader, ere this, that "vavasour" in medieval English usage is scarcely to be distinguished from "franklin." Indeed, I see no reason for attempting to do so. Chaucer's Franklin was a vavasour, and doubtless all franklins were vavasours. The two words, both of which indicate a general social condition, and were in no sense titles, appear to be interchangeable. The rarity of their appearance in documents is due, I feel sure, to the fact that they were not very explicit. There is no doubt in the world, however, that a man who could properly be described by them held a very honorable status in the realm. Chaucer's Franklin was a member of that class of landed gentry which was already old in the fourteenth century and which has never felt the lack of any higher title than gentleman, though from it have come, first and last, most of the men who have made England great.

It is possible that the designation of franklin was less well considered in the sixteenth century than it had been earlier. Edmund Dudley's *The Tree of Commonwealth,* which was written in 1509-10, lists as members of the commons "merchantes, craftesmen and artificers, laborers, franklins, grasiers, farmers, tyllers, and other generallie the people of this realme." Evidently Dudley did not place franklins high in the social scale, and indeed made his opinion even clearer by going on to say that "substanciall merchantes, the welthie grasiers and farmers" are "chief of theis folkes."[62] Yet the wealth of franklins is emphasized in two plays of the second half of the century, as has been pointed out to me by my colleague Professor Thorp. In *The Interlude of Wealth*

[61] *ibid.,* p. 92.

[62] Edn. 1859, pp. 19-20.

and Health from about 1557 they are coupled with men of law as wealthy; and in *All for Money*, a morality by Thomas Lupton (1578), a figure called Nichol-never-out-of-the-Law comes on the stage "like a riche frankeline."[63]

Whatever happened later, the social status of the franklin with whom we are concerned is not in doubt. The cloud on the life of the white-bearded, ruddy gentleman whom Chaucer pictured so vividly was not that he was baulked of founding a family, but that an honorable line seemed liable to extinction in the person of his ne'er-do-well son. If he spoke of "gentilesse"—and he uttered the word but once, outside his tale—it was simply because he was at the moment so much impressed by the contrast between the Knight's son and his own. The point of Harry Bailly's interruption seems to me to be that he was impatient and fearful of an old gentleman's garrulity. It is unfortunate that we have not his comment when the story was ended, for he might then have been less rude. Truly seen, the Franklin is as appealing a figure as any other among the pilgrims. The Host was clearly in the wrong when he mistook the cry of distress wrung from the heart of a proud old man for the beginning of a senile flood of words. That the Franklin was both proud and sure of himself is shown by his good-natured acquiescence at Harry Bailly's interruption. He went forward straightway with his tale, which turned on "gentilesse," to be sure, but on "gentilesse" in its highest phase. When all is said, where in literature can be found a better brief sketch of a true gentleman than Chaucer drew in his picture of the Franklin?[64]

[63] *Malone Society Reprints*, 1907, lines 512-513; *Tudor Facsimile Texts*, 1910.

[64] This chapter is the revised form of a paper first printed in *PMLA* (XLI, 1926).

iii · the vicious pardoner

Of the "wel nyne and twenty" pilgrims who assembled at the Tabard Inn and put themselves under the guidance and control of Harry Bailly, the Pardoner has been the one about whom and about whose performance the most sharply differing opinions have been expressed. The complexities of his personality are perhaps not greater than those of that superbly imagined creature, the Wife of Bath, but they are more difficult to understand. The fault, if it be a fault, is to some extent Chaucer's. If he had taken pains at one or two points to explain a little more carefully, no one could fail to see what he meant, and possibly he might have straightened out at least one apparent inconsistency. It is questionable, however, whether the corrections would have been worth while. The Pardoner is a murky figure and is doubtless best viewed against a murky sky. *Hamlet* would be no greater, even if in some ways more intelligible, if Shakespeare had left us a "definitive" edition with all the rough places made smooth.

Yet not wholly from unworthy curiosity we should like to have a few questions answered. We should like to know, first of all, whether the sketch of the Pardoner in the General Prologue was written before his dramatic introduction at the end of the *Physician's Tale,* but we have no clear evidence from the manuscripts on what is, though it has never been so recognized, a point of very considerable importance. The two passages are, at all events, closely connected. In the General Prologue the Pardoner is said to be riding (though the pilgrims are also said to be assembled at the Tabard Inn) with the ill-favored and rascally Summoner, who had not only garlanded himself but set a "cake" up before him as a buckler. It is expressly stated that the garland was

> As greet as it were for an ale-stake.[1]

The cake, according to the normal use of the term until very much later, would have been a "cake of bread," or in our terms a circular, flattened loaf. The emphasis on the Summoner's two pieces of equipment is unmistakable. Without them the account of him is sufficiently complete—marvellously so: his grotesque appearance, his deplorable personal habits, and even something of his opinions. Then at the end, most unexpectedly, we are told about the garland and the edible buckler. If the lines are an appendix, their addition did nothing to injure the detailed and altogether admirable description of the Summoner. Their unexpectedness, moreover, adds to their force.[2]

Oddly enough, though Chaucer made the Summoner's garland and his cake so conspicuous, and anticipated later action by stating in the General Prologue that he rode with the Pardoner, readers appear, as I have said, to have paid little attention to the picture so sketched. In regard to this the poet cannot be accused of any vagueness of statement. Whether he wrote the passage in the Prologue in anticipation of what was to happen at the close of the *Physician's Tale,* or whether he went back to introduce the garland and the cake after the Physician-Pardoner link was written, the two passages explain one another. The action in the latter scene is sufficiently plain. Harry Bailly is so moved by the piteous story of Virginius and Virginia that only "triacle" or "moyste and corny ale" or a "myrie tale" can save him from what he seems to call blunderingly a "cardy-

[1] *CT,* 1,667.

[2] That they were added seems to me most probable from the discrepancies between the sketch of the Pardoner and his discourse later on.

nacle."[3] The mocking Pardoner is willing to provide the required "myrthe or japes,"

> "But first," quod he, "heere at this ale-stake
> I wol bothe drynke, and eten of a cake."[4]

The cake is right at hand. Why, indeed, should the Summoner have been provided with such a grotesque and inconvenient object except to serve the Pardoner for precisely this reference? As for the drink, there is good reason for believing that he was not intended to get it from any other source than his own flask, and also that he was already rather tipsy. He had only to reach across and break off a bit of his companion's loaf, which would be in itself an effective gesture, and take a swig of his own ale at the same time. The Summoner with his garland provided the appropriate ale-stake. No wonder that "thise gentils" cried out:

> Nay, let hym telle us of no ribaudye!

His quality and condition would have been only too evident.

But, it may be urged, the inn on the Canterbury road where the pilgrims stopped for refreshment has long been a well-known if not precisely located landmark. It has even been pictured. It has been so taken for granted by commentators and editors that it has become solidly established in the minds of almost everyone. It is a literary legend and like many other legends both sacred and profane is believed no less firmly because there is no warrant for the belief. The only thing suggestive of an inn is the ale-stake, and the ale-stake cannot possibly be anything other than the Summoner's headgear. However great the shock to cherished feelings, the public-house must be eliminated. But, someone may still say, does not the Pardoner's statement

[3] Unless the fault was scribal.

[4] *CT*, VI,321-322.

that he must both eat and drink while he brings to memory "some honest thyng" imply reflection at an inn, even though there is no explicit reference to an inn in the text? There is the Pardoner's stimulating draught to be accounted for.

In view of the exhibition which immediately follows, any such argument has no force. The Pardoner needed little or no time to search his memory for a moral story. As a matter of fact, he does not begin a tale as he was expected to do but instead plunges into an extraordinary confession of evil practices which is explicable only on the supposition that he has already drunk unwisely. This can be demonstrated, I think, by an unprejudiced analysis of his extended prologue in contrast to the postponed narrative. To that we shall come shortly. In passing, it is well to observe that Chaucer sketches another scene of ambulatory inebriety in the prologue of the *Manciple's Tale*.[5] In that instance, to be sure, the Cook tumbles off his horse and has to be hoisted into the saddle again, but he is then able to proceed. He is worse off than the Pardoner, that is all. And there is no point in our asking how the Pardoner or any other pilgrim could be heard by his companions while discoursing. Chaucer pictured life faithfully but never troubled about literal accuracy of detail when the detail was of no importance.

Before looking precisely at the Pardoner's harangue, we ought to see what Chaucer says of the man's personal characteristics. The account is seemingly inconsistent in some particulars as between the sketch in the General Prologue and his later introduction. For example, he declares in his confession that he will "have a joly wenche in every toun,"[6] yet the earlier description says:[7]

[5] *CT*, IX,4-50.
[6] *CT*, VI,453.
[7] *CT*, I,689-691.

> No berd hadde he, ne nevere sholde have;
> As smothe it was as it were late shave.
> I trowe he were a geldyng or a mare.

Chaucer's surmise about him can be reconciled with his own statement just quoted only on the assumption that he was a natural eunuch rather than a castrate. The former, according to authorities cited by Professor Curry,[8] were thought to desire the company of women. It would perhaps be inquiring too curiously to ask whether Chaucer distinguished clearly between *eunuchus ex nativitate* and a "geldyng." The alternative surmise that the Pardoner might be a "mare" has escaped comment, as far as I know. Does it mean that he might be suspected of being homosexual? I can find no such definition of the word *mare,* but I am unwilling to believe that Chaucer used it idly. In any event, Chaucer pretends to no expert knowledge. His surmise was based on appearance: the effeminacy of the Pardoner's smooth yellow hair and his dress, the quality of his voice.

Harry Bailly, it is evident, drew no such inference. In his brutal retort to the Pardoner when invited to be the first to confess his sins, he takes for granted the existence of "coillons," which he would like to destroy. There is less positive evidence to be drawn from the rude interruption of the Wife of Bath by the Pardoner.[9] When he says that he had been thinking of marriage but will be withheld by her exposition of a husband's marital duties, she treats his impudence with scorn and a pointed reference to his tipsiness.

> Nay, thou shalt drynken of another tonne,
> Er that I go, shal savoure wors than ale.

She dislikes his manners, it is clear, and despises him for an

[8] W. C. Curry, *Chaucer and the Mediaeval Sciences,* 1926, p. 58.
[9] *CT,* III,163-171.

effeminate creature, but she does not deny his possible virility.[10]

Probably we should be content with these slightly vague references and conclude that Chaucer meant his Pardoner to be sexually abnormal in one way or another, but did not bother to be specific. One statement about him in the preliminary sketch, however, is impossible to reconcile with his later performance. We are told:

> A voys he hadde as smal as hath a goot.[11]

The voice of the goat is notoriously thin and quavering, as everyone knows. Yet he himself says that when he preaches in church, he takes pains

> to han a hauteyn speche,
> And rynge it out as round as gooth a belle.[12]

Many of the most effective passages in his discourse, moreover, are so orotund in tone that they could not well be delivered except by a voice of depth and range. He sang "Com hider, love, to me" "ful loude," but without further specification. We have to fall back, I think, on the supposition, which is in no way unreasonable, that Chaucer's conception of the Pardoner developed considerably after he wrote the General Prologue. Any little discrepancies are of themselves unimportant, but they are an index to the growth in the poet's imagination of the fantastic creature who was to become one of the most sinister yet morally convincing figures in all literature.

There have been repeated attempts during the past half century and more to show that his discourse is essentially a sermon, a sermon conforming to the established pattern. Unfortunately there is much in it unbecoming to a sermon, and by any analysis it lacks orderliness. If a sermon, it has

10 See G. G. Sedgewick, *MLQ,* I (1940),445-446.

11 *CT,* I,688.

12 *CT,* VI,330-331.

split at the seams. I do not propose to review the explanations which others have made, pointing out what seem to me the errors in each and thus attempting to arrive at the truth by a process of elimination. Instead, with all proper deference to my predecessors, whose conclusions seem to me largely mistaken, I shall invite attention to what the Pardoner is reported to have said.

He plunges at once into a brazen avowal of his hypocritical preaching, which he says is always from the text *Radix malorum est Cupiditas.* In the passage immediately following (335-343) he gives evidence for the first time of the inebriety which is so skillfully intimated by Chaucer. He says that he displays all the bulls by which he is protected while carrying on "Cristes hooly werk," but he is unable to control his tongue and instances far too many bulls for even the best-provided pardoner to have in his possession:

> Bulles of popes and of cardynales,
> Of patriarkes and bishopes I shewe.

Nonsense, of course, and with an interlarded line,

> And after that thanne telle I forth my tales,

which completes the confusion. Read aloud, the passage suggests even more plainly than to the eye that the speaker is in the talkative stage of intoxication.

He goes on to explain shamelessly the false relics he carries. When sober, such a rascal as he might in bravado admit that he had the shoulder-bone of a sheep, but surely it would not be "of a hooly Jewes sheep." (351) Even the explanation sometimes offered that by the holy Jew was meant an unnamed Hebrew prophet or patriarch[13] does not help matters. What character of the Old Testament had a sheep so endowed with magical powers? Furthermore, the holy

[13] Skeat, Manly, Robinson, et al.

Jew reappears a dozen lines later (364), teaching "oure eldres" to drink fasting the water of a well in which the sheep's shoulder-bone had been washed. This is supreme effrontery, but it is supremely muddled effrontery.

The histrionic temper, without which the Pardoner could not have had the success of which he boasts, is no less operative because out of control. His eloquence mounts as he continues to extol the virtues of the water in which the bone of the holy Jew's sheep has been washed. It will cure the most well-founded jealousy, even though the guilty wife had had two or three priests as lovers. The malice in this is genuine, however consciously false the rest. Swept along on the tide of his own drunken eloquence as he is, it is hard to say to what extent the Pardoner is conscious of what he is doing. Between ale and histrionism he is almost a somnambulist.

If any wight be in this chirche now,

he cries (378), and yet is capable of preparing an ingenious trap for a supposed congregation. The men or women who have sinned so deeply that shame keeps them from confession will not have the power or the grace to make an offering to the relics, but all others will appear and be shriven.

At this point (389) there is a sudden deflation of mood, as if the Pardoner had wakened to reality, and he proceeds to reveal with unsparing emphasis the methods by which he makes a fat income year by year. He is the drunkard whom most of us have met at one time or another, who calmly and sometimes tearfully tells all to a stranger casually encountered. Only this drunkard is an actor of talent and is aware of his gifts.

Thanne peyne I me to strecche forth the nekke,
And est and west upon the peple I bekke,
As dooth a dowve sittynge on a berne. (395-397)

He is utterly cynical and repeatedly asserts that his one intent in preaching against avarice is to get each and everyone

> To yeven hir pens, and namely unto me. (402)

He does not care, as he says of his audiences with the aptness of phrase which is one of his gifts,

> Though that hir soules goon a-blakeberyed. (406)

There is no confusion in this analysis and little evidence of personal feeling. He enumerates various evil motives from which sermons are preached, and only in mentioning hate is he stirred to illustrate how he can damage an enemy from the pulpit. In this he again reveals a touch of the malice which is one of his more sinister characteristics. He then insists (423-434) that he constantly preaches against the vice which is his own—avarice, coming back to it with drunken repetitiousness. As he himself remarks:

> Of this mateere it oghte ynogh suffise. (434)

It occurs to him, perhaps because of his promise to tell a story, that in preaching he uses exemplary tales to please the common people and—inevitably—to get money from them. He grows passionate in declaring that he will get for himself wealth in every form, and in a crescendo which is reflected in the verse he shouts:

> I wol have moneie, wolle, chese, and whete,
> Al were it yeven of the povereste page,
> Or of the povereste wydwe in a village,
> Al sholde hir children sterve for famyne.
> Nay, I wol drynke licour of the vyne
> And have a joly wenche in every toun. (448-453)

As has already been intimated, the last boast may perhaps be the bravado of unfulfilled desire. And suddenly he changes his tone to one of candid good-fellowship. Ah, yes, you wish me to tell a tale. By God, I'll give you something you will like: one of the moral stories I use in preaching.

He begins thereupon with a vivid but not wholly coherent account of a group of young folk in Flanders who are given over to riot and folly, frequenting brothels and taverns. They eat and drink too much; they curse abominably; and they laugh at one another's wickedness. (463-476) This is told in a heightened style suitable to the pulpit, into which the Pardoner falls as a matter of course. His imagined group becomes momentarily so real to him that with the reference to their laughter he sees them gathered in a vaguely conceived tavern, whither throng well-made acrobats and girls selling fruit and waffles, and singers with harps, all of whom are devil's ministers inciting to lechery. (472-482) In spite of its homiletic force, which Chaucer has wonderfully instrumented, this is not quite clearly imagined, as I have said. We drift with the female tempters into a tavern which must be in Flanders because the young rioters are said to belong there, but which has no other distinguishing feature. Though the Pardoner certainly had some story in mind (or Chaucer for him), his approach to it is so curiously indirect that we are not surprised when he breaks it off altogether. The tale is really never begun, and it has nothing whatever to do with the superb story which the Pardoner in due course relates. The efforts of critics to weld the two narratives have inevitably been unsuccessful and have resulted only in confusion.

The Pardoner is now distracted by his own reference to drunkenness. With the lack of control characteristic of him except in the tale proper, he develops with amusing particularity the catastrophes which have overtaken drunkards and gluttons. He follows this vein, indeed, longer than any other. (485-588) Such anecdotes and allusions would have been part of his repertory as a preacher, even though he has said that his theme was always avarice. His own pleasantly inebriated state not only heightens the satire but increases the eloquence of his denunciation. Lot and Herod and Attila all paid the penalty for their gluttony in meat or drink; and their fates stir the orator to extremest pity for the degeneracy of man.

> Allas! the shorte throte, the tendre mouth,
> Maketh that est and west and north and south,
> In erthe, in eir, in water, men to swynke
> To gete a glotoun deyntee mete and drynke! (517-520)

Yet he describes the processes of cookery with a gusto which betrays his eager concern with food, and he so thoroughly dramatizes the state of the drunkard that it is impossible to tell whether he is consciously mimicking inebriate behavior or merely letting himself go with all inhibitions discarded. He certainly is illustrating most aptly his own judgment:

> For dronkenesse is verray sepulture
> Of mannes wit and his discrecioun. (558-559)

Even his jest about the effect of cheap and strong Spanish wines on other wines stored near them is the kind of thing which would be current among patrons of taverns, but would be singularly inappropriate to a sermon; and we must not forget that the Pardoner is supposed to be reporting the manner and the matter of his preaching. On the other hand, the buffoonery of

> And thurgh thy dronke nose semeth the soun
> As though thou seydest ay "Sampsoun, Sampsoun!"
> (553-554)

might well have been used by him hundreds of times when stimulated only by the sound of his own voice and the consciousness of an audience. Another of his habitual tricks as a popular preacher, no doubt, was his correction of a word which might possibly be misunderstood.

Nat Samuel, but Lamuel, seye I.

He breaks off (588) with one of his sudden descents from absurd and inflated eloquence to common sense.

Namoore of this, for it may wel suffise.

In a somewhat perfunctory way he then attacks gambling as, severally, the mother of lies, deceit, and false oaths, of blasphemy, manslaughter, and waste of property and time. The shame which comes from it he illustrates by two anecdotes from his stock in trade. He then finally speaks "a word or two" about violations of the second commandment of the Decalogue, or the third as reckoned in the English Bible. The dubious argument that the prohibition of false and idle swearing is more stringent than that of homicide or "many a cursed thyng" because it precedes the others in the table of the Law may be regarded, I think, as a muddled burlesque of such distinctions as an entirely sober preacher might draw. (645-647) Reminiscence might have supplied the sharply dramatized scene (651-655) of a quarrel between players at hazard, which in five lines sums up the evils of gambling more effectively than much exhortation would do. Like the best of *genre* pictures it reveals both the immediate scene and its background. The Pardoner's histrionic gift here shows at its best. His rambling discourse comes to a brilliant end.

But, sires, now wol I telle forth my tale. (660)

Having finished a more or less complete confession of his shocking depravity, he becomes aware again of his promise to tell a story.

The commentators who have urged that his discourse is patterned on the conventional sermon of the medieval period, with the tale itself serving as the customary *exemplum,* have encountered very serious difficulties. Granted that the

Pardoner is a creature of unexampled effrontery, he is by his own account and by the evidence of his performance a gifted pulpit orator. If he were bent on preaching a sermon or even making an impudent burlesque of one, he surely would have been able to give it a satisfactory formal arrangement, or Chaucer would have done so for him. Yet he follows no plan. He does not even move forward, but instead rambles from topic to topic as one thing suggests another. He begins by saying that avarice is his sole theme as a preacher, but he deserts it at once for his confession and returns to it only to emphasize his own wickedness. He recalls his engagement to tell a story, but drops the tale after a few lines and drifts into a denunciation first of gluttony and then of gambling. This is no illustration of medieval sermonizing, though the speaker is a trained preacher and incidentally displays both knowledge of homiletic materials and tricks of his profession.

Nor will the Pardoner's impudent rascality explain his tirade. A man so depraved and so intent on getting for himself every possible creature comfort would not, unless his natural inhibitions were suspended, have stripped himself naked in mixed company. He would have been too canny for that. His loss of control, and therefore his whole performance, can be explained only by understanding that he was tipsy, and tipsy to the point of not caring what he said and indeed not being altogether conscious of it. No cup or two of ale at a wayside tavern would have brought him to the state which Chaucer suggests with such marvelous skill. Drink has not only loosened his tongue, as has sometimes been admitted by critics, but it has thoroughly befuddled him.

When he comes at length to the point of telling his "moral tale," Chaucer as is wholly right takes over. He could not, and did not, let any hint of drunken buffoonery mar the grim and tragic irony of the narrative. To that end he sacrificed dramatic propriety. At least he did so if we regard the surface only. The Pardoner could not give the story the form it has, or the moral force. He would spoil the tale if it were delivered in the vein proper to him. Yet as shaped by Chaucer—as all the tales really are, of course—the dramatic irony of its attribution to the Pardoner is not lost. In his soberer hours that "ful vicious man," who was nevertheless intelligent, might well have appreciated this.

What I am not wise enough to explain satisfactorily is how Chaucer shifted the tone from dramatic verisimilitude to dramatic formalism without breaking the continuity. It is the voice of the Pardoner which goes on, but of a Pardoner cleansed and elevated. There are the same sharply outlined images, the same verse rhythms accommodated to natural speech at one point and raised to passionate utterance at another. The tale does not clash with what has gone before. Yet much of its power lies in the restraint with which terrible events are chronicled and in the beautiful precision of their inexorable movement. It could not be more different in these respects from the scrambled tirade by which it is preceded. The skill with which the two are adapted to one another without sacrificing their individual qualities is beyond praise.

There is little need any longer to stress the merits of the narrative attributed to the Pardoner. Everyone knows its transcendent worth: the compression and understatement by which the tensity of mood is maintained; the irony by which the three searchers for the pleasures of life find death, while the old man who may be Death himself cannot escape a semblance of life; the sense of mystery, which is the mystery of fate and free will. It is great because it has a meaning beyond its immediate meaning.

As I have already said, the scene in the Flanders tavern can have nothing whatever to do with the tale of the three rioters in search of death, and the attempt to connect the two is futile. The tavern in Flanders is riotously gay, filled with young folk who indulge in every kind of folly. There are also the attendants, the sellers of food and drink, the entertainers, and the providers of entertainment. The house must have been very full. In contrast, the other tavern is a melancholy place, deserted by everyone except the host, a boy, and the three lonely customers. It is early morning in a time of pestilence, and the three men have settled down to drink but not in a spirit of gaiety, we are certain. The air is heavy with evil portent, and the mood is not lightened when the corpse of an old acquaintance is carried by. No two scenes could be more different than this and that. Critics have been led astray, no doubt, by the abruptness with which the Pardoner begins his story of the search for death.

> Thise riotoures thre of whiche I telle,

he says, though there has been no previous mention of them. The phrase "of whiche I telle" refers, of course, to the present and the future and not to the past, and it serves as a link with the preceding anecdote of the quarrelsome gamesters.

At the end of the tale the Pardoner may be said to resume his discourse in person, for Chaucer no longer orders and restrains the wild torrent of his eloquence. Though the tale has taken the place of the customary *exemplum* in what the Pardoner by this time seems to have come momentarily to regard as a sermon, it interrupts his personal performance, which has turned out to be confessional. And now he is at his histrionic but slightly incoherent best. (895)

> O cursed synne of alle cursednesse!
> O traytours homycide, O wikkednesse!
> O glotonye, luxurie, and hasardrye!

> Thou blasphemour of Crist with vileynye
> And othes grete, of usage and of pride!

This is the rhetoric of the spell-binder to whom sense matters little if the sound is right. It is so earnest in tone that one might almost believe the speaker to be self-convinced. Self-forgetful to the extent of being lost in his part we must certainly believe him to be, else he would not go on to attempt the sale of his pardons. He had adequately explained their nature. Now he wishes to free his auditors from the sin of avarice, which is a return to the theme with which he began.

Then his intoxication, whether with ale or with his own acting, appears suddenly to end. "And lo, sires, thus I preche," he says flatly, and goes on in three lines (916-918) to speak for the first time like an honest man.

> And Jhesu Crist, that is oure soules leche,
> So graunte yow his pardoun to receyve,
> For that is best; I wol yow nat deceyve.

These are words of truth and soberness, and puzzling words to be spoken by the Pardoner as he has revealed himself. In spite of their difficulty, however, we should be unwise to assume that they are "out of character." The Pardoner is Chaucer's creation, and everyone recognizes him to be a very great fictional creation. His unexpected and momentary exhibition of decency must be accepted without reserve, since his author attributed it to him. We may speculate as much as we please about this white spot on his cloak of infamy, but we cannot escape it. Just there, briefly, the Pardoner showed that he knew the difference between good and evil, between truth and falsehood. One may guess that Chaucer put the words in his mouth because he meant him to be a human being. He was a very wicked man, but no devil.

His immediate return thereafter to cynical effrontery is what one would expect, for such effrontery is his habitual mood. Sobered, and no doubt conscious of his self-betrayal, he becomes more impudent than ever in offering his unholy wares for sale. Perhaps there is mockery in his most blasphemous proposal of all:

> Or elles taketh pardoun as ye wende,
> Al newe and fressh at every miles ende,

but mockery would make it no less odious. In retrospect, or regarded as a fictional character, the Pardoner is so amusing that he fails to shock us by his wickedness. His immediate effect would inevitably be different. Otherwise the Host would not have flared into such hot anger when the Pardoner suggested that he be the first to get a pardon as the one "moost envoluped in synne." The utter grossness of his retort is the measure of his disgust at the Pardoner's brazen hypocrisy. One cannot suppose that Harry Bailly would ordinarily have been so sensitive about a reference to his human frailties, but his wrath on this occasion is understandable. It would have been like being attacked by a rat. The Pardoner's speechless anger when flooded by the Host's obscenity is also easy to understand. Only by the intervention of the Knight could peace be restored.

In what I have written I have consciously avoided, except in one or two instances, any reference to opinions about the Pardoner and his discourse which have been expressed in the past. It has seemed to me more profitable to attempt a fresh and careful reading of Chaucer's text rather than to dispute the conclusions of others. I have wished to make a positive instead of a negative approach to the problem. This does not mean that I have ignored what others have written, or wished to treat it with disrespect, since views which I believe mistaken have sometimes suggested to me more satisfactory explanations. Indeed, though my interpretation may appear a very radical departure from some long-accepted ideas, it owes much to the studies of the past decades.

IV · SOME DOMINANT IDEAS OF THE WIFE OF BATH

THE extensive but not too well-digested learning which the Wife of Bath acquired from her fifth husband has latterly a little obscured, it seems to me, both the outline of her tale and some facets of her rich personality. Recent studies[1] have accomplished a great deal by way of revealing what was in Chaucer's mind when he concocted for the garrulous dame of his invention her flood of recollection and bold defiance of anti-feminism. They have told us rather less about Dame Alison, who is at the same time the propagandist of love and in some ways its victim.

Chaucer was fully aware of the incongruous elements in courtly love, which was essentially an attempt to elevate the love of men and women by undermining the foundations of society. He did not deride it, as he showed in the *Franklin's Tale,* but he saw, as all too few persons have learned even six centuries later, that reverence and forbearance are consistent with the warmest human passion. He also saw the follies into which sex plunges both young and old, but he viewed them tolerantly as absurdities inherent in nature, accepting them as amusing displays of an aspect of life which cannot be ignored. The Wife of Bath had the same validity for him as Custance and Cecilie and Dorigen —neither more nor less. Though she could not properly be endowed with any understanding of the subtleties of

[1] See particularly G. R. Coffman, "Chaucer and Courtly Love Once More," *Speculum,* XX (1945),43-50; M. Schlauch, "The Marital Dilemma in the *Wife of Bath's Tale,*" *PMLA,* LXI (1946),416-430; A. K. Moore, "The Pardoner's Interruption of the *Wife of Bath's Prologue,*" *MLQ,* X (1949),49-57; B. F. Huppé, "Rape and Woman Sovereignty in the *Wife of Bath's Tale,*" *MLN,* LXIII (1948),378-381.

courtly love, she could by her native wit and experience arrive at the conclusion that "gentilesse cometh fro God allone."

Miss Schlauch has argued persuasively that the marital dilemma propounded in the tale of the *Loathly Lady* as the Wife of Bath tells the story stems from a tradition "of social satire and of theology." She has rightly stressed the close connection between the prologue and the tale, the latter serving as a further illustration of the experiences which Dame Alison has undergone. No one can dispute, I think, the main contentions of Professor Coffman and Professor Schlauch. Chaucer was using courtly and theological notions for purposes of human comedy. He had his own opinions, it is clear, but in the utterances of the Wife of Bath he was not arguing, much less dogmatizing. No artist has ever been more successful in seeming to set a fictional personage free to abound in his or her own sense, and he nowhere more successfully than with the Wife of Bath. Though he was in control, he managed to make what she said appear altogether spontaneous and self-directed.

She impresses herself so strongly on the reader that we are in danger of treating her as if in her time she had had actual being, as if she were something else than a creature imagined by Chaucer. In thinking about his characters as in thinking about the fictional people whom we encounter in the works of certain other great artists we must take pains to discriminate between the figure created and the creator. I am not sure that in the recent discussion of the Wife of Bath and her *Tale,* fruitful though it has been, this distinction has always been observed. Chaucer made Dame Alison embellish her autobiography with borrowed learning and reconstruct her borrowed tale to fit her own obsessions. The opinions she held were truly hers, though Chaucer gave them to her.

Sources upon which he might have drawn for the tale

as it stands have been so well explored[2] that there is no doubt of its being a skillful amalgamation of two stories: that of a man's success in finding the answer to a riddle and that of a hag transformed by love. We have every right to suppose that Chaucer himself combined the two themes, and combined them in such a way as to make the refashioned tale supremely suitable to the Wife of Bath as he had conceived her. Into her manner of story-telling we must a little later inquire, but first it will be well to consider the strange way in which the tale begins. The scene is laid:

> In th'olde dayes of the Kyng Arthour,
> Of which that Britons speken greet honour.

A knight of that charmed circle was returning from sport with his falcons when:

> allone as she was born,
> He saugh a mayde walkynge hym biforn,
> Of which mayde anon, maugree hir heed,
> By verray force, he rafte hire maydenhed.

This sensational opening, so out of key with conceptions of Arthurian romance both medieval and modern, has for some reason into which we need not inquire awakened almost no curiosity on the part of Chaucerian scholars. Apparently they have not been disturbed by the knight's behavior. As far as I know, only Professor Huppé in the paper already cited has noticed the significance of the sordid detail; and he, I believe, has not arrived at the correct explanation of its presence. He would have us understand that Chaucer introduced it to illustrate the subleties of courtly love. The young knight is protected by the queen because the girl he raped was a peasant, a fact which without exempting him from the death penalty brings him un-

[2] For a judicious selection see B. J. Whiting in *Sources and Analogues of Chaucer's Canterbury Tales,* ed. Bryan and Dempster, pp. 223-268.

der the jurisdiction of the court of love. The case must there be decided. Since "rape—even of a peasant girl—is not praiseworthy: it is behavior which, though excusable, is a violation of the courtly principle of measure,"[3] he has to be taught the basic principle of the code—the sovereignty of woman. Hence he is required to find out what women most desire.

I must confess that I do not see why, if the rape of a peasant girl is a venial offence, it should be taken so seriously, with "swich pursute" and "swich clamour" even to Arthur's court. We are not told by Chaucer why the queen and her ladies beg the king to give the knight a chance for his life. Mr. Huppé's surmise that the young man would not have fallen into his error if he had been properly instructed, and therefore is preserved in order that he may be taught, is not convincing. After all, as the Wife of Bath could have told Mr. Huppé, ignorance of the prevailing social code has never been the normal cause of sexual misbehavior. The question of women's sovereignty has little relevance to the act. Furthermore, the assumption that the girl in the story was a peasant is ill-supported both by Chaucer and by Andreas Capellanus, to whom Mr. Huppé appeals. Chaucer calls her simply a "mayde" without further designation, while Andrew in his discussion of the methods of making love to a girl of the lower classes is clearly describing seduction rather than rape.[4] In Dame Alison's story there is no equivocation, I think: the knight is guilty of rape, which is not even suggested in any of the analogues which have been found.

If we remember who is supposed to be telling the story, we ought not to be surprised at the grotesque absurdity of

[3] Huppé, *op.cit.*, p. 380.

[4] Andreas Capellanus, *De Amore*, I,xi. After a course of flattery the young man may gain his object *violento . . . amplexu*, but only because by the employment *modicae saltem coactionis* the girl's native modesty may be overcome.

beginning a tale of *gentilesse* with rape. Perhaps the very aptness of its introduction by Dame Alison has kept it from the notice of critics. The Wife of Bath is sex-obsessed, as she has sufficiently demonstrated in her prologue. It was a characteristic stroke of genius on Chaucer's part to have her modify a romantic story of Arthurian days by giving it an earthy tone. Only a woman whose thoughts dwelt as did hers on the pleasures of the flesh would have imagined the incident. Yet the incident does fit cunningly into the structure of the narrative, out of key though it is when considered by itself: the marital dilemma which later confronts the knight is a question of the lady's loyal chastity with physical repulsiveness on the one hand or her physical beauty with the chance of unfaithfulness on the other. There is irony in having the knight's act of unbridled lust lead to such a dilemma, but there is suitability. There is no logical connection, indeed, between the beginning of the story and its end except the one just pointed out. Though unobtrusive, it has an important effect on the reader, who feels without perhaps knowing why a harmony of structure in the fittingly rambling discourse. A tighter organization would not have been appropriate to the garrulous story-teller. Even her somewhat pedantic analysis of gentilesse has a fine irony in view of the young knight's earlier behavior.

Although by no means all the *Canterbury Tales* are especially fitted to the pilgrims relating them, the dramatic adaptation in a few instances is so perfect that even their manner of speech is reflected in the verse. This is eminently true of the Wife of Bath. Chaucer could adapt the five-measure couplet to many ends. For the speech of the Wife of Bath he made it heavy-footed though with frequent sharp turns to indicate the play of her satiric wit. The accent of speech is preserved throughout both prologue and tale. It is notoriously difficult to describe the subtle variations of tempo and rhythm, but Chaucer has suggested

Dame Alison's utterance so plainly that any moderately competent reading will make it heard for what it is. Her reminiscences, her sharp passages at arms with the Pardoner and the Friar, and her story of the lady whose youth was marvellously restored are so naturally spoken that we seem to be in her living presence. There never was a clearer case to illustrate the suspension of disbelief.

Yet neither she, nor Chaucer for her, strains after verisimilitude. Certainly nothing could be more implausible than the string of quotations from various antifeminist tracts and poems with which she lards her prologue. We assume that she borrowed her learning from Jankyn, her fifth husband, to whose instruction indeed she attributed her knowledge of some of the passages, and we may assume also from the vividness with which she describes scenes of her past life that she was gifted with total recall; yet we cannot deny that her memory is made somewhat unnaturally tenacious. In other respects her prologue is altogether matter-of-fact, which gives point to the extravagance of her quotations and to the continuous irony of making her, the arch-feminist, disclose so devastatingly the dangers of marriage.

It has sometimes been argued that she is a disappointed and disillusioned woman, having looked for happiness in vain. That she has had disappointments cannot be denied. After all her experiments in matrimony death removed the one husband who had given her complete satisfaction. But disillusioned she cannot properly be called.

> An housbonde I wol have, I wol nat lette,[5]

she says, though her acknowledged age makes a sixth marriage improbable. Perhaps, as has often been remarked, the vigor of her argument in praise of the free indulgence of sexual appetites in marriage is evidence that she regrets

[5] *CT*, III,154.

her loss of youth, but it certainly does not indicate any real dissatisfaction with the pleasures of the flesh. She is still a hearty creature, greatly preoccupied with sex but not to the exclusion of other interests.

> She koude muchel of wandrynge by the weye.[6]

It matters little whether we are to believe that she or anybody like her had thrice journeyed to Jerusalem, as Chaucer tells us casually in his initial sketch. He establishes at all events her love of adventure, which is of a piece with her experiments with marriage and, if we view it rightly, with her tale.

First of all, we ought to bear in mind that the story is not to be taken too seriously. She says:

> But that I praye to al this compaignye,
> If that I speke after my fantasye,
> As taketh not agrief of that I seye;
> For myn entente is nat but for to pleye.[7]

So in a light mood and without apology she begins a fairy-tale. In the old days of King Arthur this land was rife with fairies.

> The elf-queene, with her joly compaignye,
> Daunced ful ofte in many a grene mede.[8]

But now, she goes on at once to say, the elves have disappeared, and in their place have come the holy friars, whose ways and works she rehearses with what we might call Rabelaisian particularity if it postdated that great artist. Both the momentary and lovely glimpse of the dancing elf-queen and the sharp irony of the attack on the friars are characteristic of her. Chaucer endowed her with sensibility, as she shows in her prologue by dwelling with satisfaction on her walks "into the feeldes" with her gossip and Jankyn;

[6] *CT*, I,467. [7] *CT*, III,189-192. [8] *CT*, III,860-861.

but common sense and preoccupation with sex are dominant in her. The friars have driven away the fairies. No incubus will attack women any more: they are safe except from friars.

With choicest irony Dame Alison goes on without a break to tell about the rape of a maiden in those good old days, not by an incubus at that but by a knight of King Arthur's court. She makes no comment to show herself aware of the irony. As has been pointed out above, she might well think the opening a most natural gambit and be oblivious to its humorous impropriety. She then becomes concerned with the riddling question which the knight is required to answer, and we with her. She is telling a fairy-tale which ends happily because, in the first place, the hero finds means to tell the queen:

> Wommen desiren have sovereynetee
> As wel over hir housbond as hir love,

and because, secondly, having married his rescuer to fulfil a promise blindly given, he allows her dominion over him. All this is "fantasy," as the Wife of Bath avers, but it meshes so firmly with what she has revealed about herself in her prologue that we know it to be an unconscious but trustworthy account of her inner life.

Instead of being an intricate bundle of oddments, as a too exclusive study of the sources used might make her appear, Dame Alison is one of the best integrated characters in fiction. The more closely one scrutinizes her words and ways, the better one sees that the contradictions in her are contradictions proper to a full-blooded human being. She is quick of tongue and sharp of wit, but she has no other interesting quality of mind except common sense, and common sense has not prevented her from making extravagant pilgrimages and marrying imprudently. Though argumentative, she is controlled by instinct and feeling rather than by reason; and she proves nothing whatever by her elaborate prologue and tale except that women can subjugate their menfolk if they will make the effort. Presumably that was what Chaucer intended to convey. She is a convinced feminist because she enjoys the sense of power that any sort of mastery can give and because she rather despises the dominant but indispensable male.

She does not captivate us by her argument, though it is always diverting, but by what she unconsciously reveals to us about herself and women in general. She does not follow a steady course in this, for her thoughts are vagrant, and she says the thing that comes to her mind from moment to moment. Yet little by little, as she rambles along through her life-history and her tale, she becomes clearer and clearer not only as an individual but as an individual who transcends her own individuality. She is a woman worth knowing.

V · The Serious Mind of Chaucer

ALTHOUGH we are told explicitly that Harry Bailly was jesting when he said that Chaucer seemed "elvyssh" in looks and attitude,[1] there has always been a lurking suspicion on the part of the poet's readers that he may have been describing himself with some justice. It is characteristic of his personal reticence that we cannot be sure. He represents himself as speaking to all the other pilgrims at the Tabard Inn, and so coming at once to be of their "fellowship," and his variously active career indicates that he had no difficulty in getting along with people of various kinds, yet he may have been modest of manner and approach for all that. The argument that the jest of the Host to which I refer "aims to bring Chaucer to his merry self again"[2] begs the question. Everyone had been sobered, we are told, by the tale which the Prioress had just finished. Whereupon the Host, as the prudent master of ceremonies, turns to Chaucer and demands "a tale of myrthe." In response we have *Sir Thopas,* one of the cleverest and most amusing literary parodies ever written, but not at all pleasing to Harry Bailly. He finds it, on the contrary, so tedious that he checks its stupid course obscenely.

In the meek response which Chaucer attributes to himself at this point by way introducing the *Tale of Melibee* he drops momentarily his role as pilgrim and refers to "this murye tale I write."[3] Neither in nor out of the framework,

[1] *CT,* VII,693-706.

[2] T. A. Knott, *MP,* VIII (1910),136.

[3] *CT,* VII,964. No variants reported by Manly-Rickert. Presumably by "murye" Chaucer meant no more than "pleasant." Any sardonic turn of the meaning is unlikely, since *Melibee* is treated throughout with the respect it deserves.

however, does he amuse the company by his jokes; and nowhere throughout the *Canterbury Tales* does he give a hint of being mirthful, great humorist though he was as author of the stories. We must agree that he was keenly observant and recognized human absurdities more fully than most men, but that does not imply that he rivalled Harry Bailly as a fun-maker. The assumption that he kept silence and assumed a downcast mien in order to report the words of the other pilgrims more accurately[4] is quite gratuitous. His reticence about himself baffles us, but it should not keep us from appreciating elements in his poetry which belie the notion of his being a blunt extrovert.

The common view of him as predominantly a jester, though a jester of genius, has tended to obscure certain elements of his art which are nevertheless very important. It has seldom been recognized, for example, that he makes particularly effective use of events quietly conceived and expressed with restraint in order to awaken the reader's pity. For his irony, which involves similar understatement and restraint, he has been frequently and deservedly praised, but his power of quickening sympathy and the softer emotions by the same means has been more or less neglected.

This is less easily understandable in view of the emphasis on compassion which runs throughout the *Canterbury Tales* and appears in some half dozen other works. As has been pointed out repeatedly, the nearly identical line

For pitee renneth soone in gentil herte

occurs thrice in the *Tales* and once in the *Legend of Good Women,* while the not very different

As gentil herte is fulfild of pitee

echoes it.[5] The phrase "pitee was to here" with one slight

[4] G. L. Kittredge, *Chaucer and His Poetry,* 1915, p. 184.

[5] *CT,* I,1761, IV,1986 (Lo, pitee—), V,479 (That pitee—); *LGW,* F 503, G 491; *CT,* II,660.

variation in order is found even oftener.[6] The attribute of pity is explicitly mentioned several times. Once it is applied to the blood of Christ,[7] and twice to the Virgin, who is called "of pitee welle" in the *A B C*,[8] and in the noble invocation based on Dante which appears at the head of the *Second Nun's Tale* pity is associated with her other great virtues.[9] The phrase "womanly pitee" is found three times,[10] "moodres pitee" and "fadres pitee" once each,[11] while the "kynges herte of pitee gan agryse" at the plight of Custance in the *Man of Law's Tale*.[12] Again, in the *Parson's Tale* we are told that "misericorde folweth pitee in parfournynge of charitable werkes."[13] Very different are the references in *The Complaint unto Pity*, in which the compassion of an unnamed lady is sought by a hopeless lover. The seventeen rhyme royal stanzas are in the convention of all such amorous verse and have little to do with the virtue of pity which Chaucer values so highly.

His exaltation of pity is closely related to his power of using restrained understatement to emphasize the pathos of some human situation. Repeatedly the plight of the innocent, of the deserted, of persons in one way or another caught inexorably by evil fortune or threatened with disaster is developed with tragic force. Only by sympathy and compassion is the dangerous life of man to be borne. The world is full of absurdities, to be sure, but there is no safety in it. The matter was admirably summarized long ago by the late Professor Root, the only scholar who to my knowledge has given due weight to pathos as an element in Chaucer's art.[14] "Troilus as he eagerly watches for the returning form of Cressid, Arcite taking his last leave of his kinsman and his love, Dorigen as she goes to keep her ter-

6 *CT*, I,2345,2878; *HF*, lines 180 and 181; *T&C*, II,1577; *LGW*, line 1249.
7 *CT*, II,452. 8 *ABC*, line 126. 9 *CT*, VIII,50-52.
10 *CT*, I,3083, VII,1745; *Lady*, line 101. 11 *CT*, VII,593, VI,211.
12 *CT*, II,614. 13 *CT*, X,805.
14 R. K. Root, *The Poetry of Chaucer*, rev. edn. 1922, p. 40.

rible tryst, Constance comforting her little son, Virginius dooming his daughter to the death that shall vindicate her honor, Griselda preparing for the wedding feast of the rival who is to supplant her, above all the matchless story of the murdered schoolboy singing his Alma Redemptoris—these show the touch of pathos in its purest form, and the list might be indefinitely extended."

This is well said, but in what follows even Professor Root did not to my mind go far enough in asserting the element of tragedy associated with the pathos. We must not be misled into thinking that nothing can properly be called tragic which does not follow the general lines of dramatic tragedy. Though we need not subscribe to medieval practice and call any story a tragedy provided the hero or heroine descends from a state of happiness to misery, we may accept as tragedy such a poem as *Troilus and Criseyde* which purports

> The double sorwe of Troilus to tellen,

even though very many of its scenes are conceived and executed in the spirit of comedy. The story would have little or no meaning if it did not display the fatal but not altogether culpable weaknesses of the hero and heroine. We shall see later, I hope, that Criseyde furnishes one of the clearest illustrations of Chaucer's tragic pathos. The play of wit and the interwoven comedy, though quantitatively large, do not blot the real pattern, which reveals the terror and the dangers to which human beings are exposed and frequently succumb.

It is true that in Chaucer a note of pity almost always softens the tone and true also that the mood of tragedy is sometimes only briefly sustained. Yet the pathos is never sentimentalized, which is only to say that its emotional appeal is grounded in nature, and it is equally free from the falsities of melodrama. If the mood is not sustained, moreover, there is no loss of dignity through the shift to comedy. Chaucer among his other gifts had a sense of fitness which seldom went wrong.

The effectiveness of his tragic pathos rests, as must always be the case, on the exactitude with which emotional tensions are imagined and recorded. When the key is set low, there must be precision, or nobody will be moved to pity, whereas the simplest phrase may have great force if it rings true. The quiet scene and the restrained utterance show tragic pathos at its best.

Consider the *Physician's Tale.* In plain terms the beauty and goodness of the Roman maiden are described. It is a sober account, though Virginia is given unstinted praise. An explicitly didactic passage of thirty lines follows and certainly does nothing to increase the emotional tension. As briefly as possible the plot of the wicked Apius and his fellow-conspirator is sketched, and Virginius is told that he must deliver his daughter to her ignominious doom. There is no heightening for effect in all this. Thereupon in one of the most poignant scenes ever pictured the father explains to Virginia that

> For love, and nat for hate, thou most be deed.

With her arms about his neck "as she was wont to do," she cries:

> Is ther no grace, is ther no remedye?

It would be hard to find anywhere a line of greater pathos, a line more revelatory of tragic horror. Her quiet plea

> That with his swerd he sholde smyte softe,

is in keeping with what has gone before. The simplicity and the very lack of stress in the brief exchange between father and daughter move us as only tragedy can do.[15]

[15] *CT,* VI,213-252.

Comparable with this in effect though interestingly different in the means employed is a scene in the *Man of Law's Tale*. The calumniated heroine is about to enter the ship in which with her little son she is to be set adrift.[16]

> Hir litel child lay wepyng in hir arm,
> And knelynge, pitously to hym she seyde,
> "Pees, litel sone, I wol do thee noon harm."
> With that hir coverchief of hir heed she breyde,
> And over his litel eyen she it leyde,
> And in hir arm she lulleth it ful faste,
> And into hevene hire eyen up she caste.

This is less direct, less simple. It is pictorial. The exquisite tenderness of the mother is shown both by her speech and by her actions. There follows immediately a prayer to the Virgin which increases the emotional tensity by its blending in melodious sound of the rhetorical devices which we associate with hymnology and supplication. The rich music of the passage captivates and uplifts us. In the stanza following the innocent child is first addressed and then the Constable, whom Custance begs, if he dare not save her son, to kiss him in his father's name. In a final stanza, still soothing her child, she cries "Farewel, housbonde routhelees!" and enters the waiting ship.[17]

The contrast between the austere simplicity of the scene in the *Physician's Tale* and the elaboration with which the departure of Custance from Northumbria is treated illustrates Chaucer's command of varying means to accomplish various ends. There is no difference in the degree of pathos. Each scene rings true. They are equally moving, but in the one case because of its sharply accentuated truth to a heartrending plight, in the other because of its equally truthful but very complex appeal to all our senses. In neither is

[16] *CT*, II,834-840.

[17] *CT*, II,868.

there any deviation from the quiet restraint which adds greatly to the emotional force of the scene.

Such tragic pathos appears again in the *Clerk's Tale*, even though Grisilde, after the culminating test of her patience, is given back her children and all her honors. More than in the story of Custance the feelings of the bystanders are used to accentuate Grisilde's heroic agony, which might otherwise be muffled by her humble acceptance of shocking mistreatment. Not until she resigns her husband to the beautiful maiden who is in reality her daughter, wishing him happiness but warning him not to try her as she has been tried, does the reader feel the real force of what she has suffered.

> "For she is fostred in hire norissynge
> Moore tendrely, and, to my supposynge,
> She koude nat adversitee endure
> As koude a povre fostred creature."[18]

Her selflessness, though it is beyond human limits, does not keep us from the profoundest pity. The tragic pathos of the situation, cumulative as it is, has nothing to do with the heroine as a natural person, since she is a bloodless figure: it is the fable itself that matters.

Somewhat different and more simply expressed is the anguish of the mother in the *Prioress' Tale*. In the very few lines devoted to her Chaucer manages to convey the sharp intensity of her suffering.

> With moodres pitee in hir brest enclosed,
> She gooth, as she were half out of hir mynde,
> To every place where she hath supposed
> By liklihede hir litel child to fynde;
> And evere on Cristes mooder meeke and kynde
> She cride—[19]

[18] *CT*, IV,1040-1043.

[19] *CT*, VII,593-598.

Though the search is so briefly related, we get the full sense of its painful course and its sad outcome. The tragic pathos of the widow's loss is enforced by the implicit parallel with the sorrow of the Mother of God, which is all the more effective because it is not put into words. The pathos is enhanced, too, by the noble music of the verse, keyed to the antiphon *O Alma redemptoris* and unsurpassed among the many passages in which Chaucer used harmonies of sound for their poetic effect. This aspect of his art, let it be said, has too often been ignored, though he was one of the great music-makers who have used the English tongue.

The episode of Arcite's death in the *Knight's Tale* shows in a most interesting way how an event of itself melancholy can be so adapted to the spirit of romance that the tragic pathos, though genuine, does not clash with the prevailing tone of the work. The progress of the mortal infection, as we should term it, which sets in after the young knight has been unhorsed in the arena, is described with great detail. His symptoms are observed with what may be called scientific accuracy, granting the difference between medical terms in the fourteenth century and the twentieth.

> Nature hath now no dominacioun.
> And certeinly, ther Nature wol nat wirche,
> Fare wel phisik! go ber the man to chirche![20]

The effect is pedestrian, and must certainly have been so intended. There follows a speech of thirty-two lines in which Arcite bids farewell to his lady and commends Palamon to her as a possible husband. It is an eloquent and passionate utterance, but the poignant feeling it evokes has little to do with Emelye or with Arcite himself. It is in the elegiac vein and does not depend for its force on the special circumstances.

[20] *CT*, I,2758-2760.

"What is this world? what asketh men to have?
Now with his love, now in his colde grave
Allone, withouten any compaignye."

The oncoming of death immediately thereafter is calmly told, as were the clinical details a little earlier.

Dusked his eyen two, and failled breeth,
But on his lady yet caste he his ye;
His laste word was, "Mercy, Emelye!"
His spirit chaunged hous and wente ther,
As I cam nevere, I kan nat tellen wher.

The tone of all this[21] is so little personalized that the pageantry of the funeral and the subsequent wedding of Emelye and Palamon follow with complete propriety. There was no flippancy in Chaucer's disclaimer of knowledge about the after-life of the young knight. He was concerned only with the interplay of temperament and fortune in the present world. To have individualized the persons involved and dramatized them further would have destroyed the atmosphere of romance which gives the poem its nobility and charm.

The "double sorwe" of Troilus, on the other hand, is the suffering of an individual who is revealed to us by his words, by his acts, and even by his reported thoughts. If he is more than an individual and has a significance beyond his own time and place, it is because he is so justly represented as an individual. We need not now concern ourselves with the method of his portrayal and the "truth to life" of this view of him and that. We need only observe that in spite of the lapse of centuries he is recognizably a young man whom a great love teaches and at length destroys. The suffering he undergoes before he wins Criseyde is real, as both Chaucer and Pandarus know, but it is

21 *CT*, I,2765-2810.

neither tragic nor pathetic. What he endured after the loss of his mistress is another matter.

Quite properly Chaucer somewhat alters the tone of the poem at the beginning of the fourth book. The disaster of which he had given warning at the start takes shape with the capture of Antenor by the Greeks. It was inevitable that to ransom him Criseyde should be sent to her father, inevitable that she should fail to keep her promise to return, and equally inevitable that she should succumb to a bold suitor like Diomede. There was nothing whatever that Troilus could do to alter the course of events. His long soliloquy on fate and free-will shows his reluctant recognition of conditioned free-will as a principle, and it rightly ends with a prayer to "almyghty Jove in trone" that he may either die or that Criseyde and he may be delivered from their distress. There is no hint of any conscious fear on his part that his lady may be faithless to him, though it has been made sufficiently evident that Pandarus disbelieves in her steadfastness; and she herself betrays some slight misgivings through the very elaboration and ingenuity of devices by which her return was to be assured. It is Troilus who stresses the difficulties and dangers—even the possibility of her being captivated by some Grecian knight, though in the event he is so firm in his loyal faith that only such proof of her infidelity as the rejected brooch can convince him.

Critics have been reluctant to approve Chaucer's own designation of his poem as a tragedy except in the medieval sense of a decline from high estate or happy fortune to some kind of misery. They have felt the stress on the transitory joys of the flesh to be so strong that his subsequent wretchedness does not make Troilus a genuinely tragic figure. There would be reason for this view if the poem fell apart and were no more than a story of passionate love ill-requited because not fully requited, and thus disastrous to the hero. It is such a story, of course, but it is much more, and it does not fall apart. The outcome is forecast in the opening lines, and the conclusion would lose its point if the happiness of the lovers in the third book were not fully explored. Only by ignoring the Boethian soliloquy of the fourth book and the tragic ironies of the fifth is it possible to argue that the *Troilus* has no meaning beyond that of frustrated passion and human frailty. It would leave out of account what we feel about the hero and what we come to understand by contemplating his experience. If we read wisely, we are satisfied at length that the laughter of Troilus when from the eighth sphere he views "this litel spot of erthe" does not come from a cynical repudiation of man's joys and sorrows but from his knowledge of a cosmic harmony in which he has his tiny share.

Troilus lacks qualities which have been traditionally associated with heroes of tragedy, and he moves through scenes which have not the texture of tragedy, but his experience is tragic quite as truly as that of any protagonist of them all. Although in our time no informed person is going to deny "high seriousness" to Chaucer, it is still necessary to assert his power not only of rising to a great argument but of developing a lofty theme in a complex pattern. If we look at the pattern of *Troilus* as a whole, which we ought to do, we find the same emotional restraint which is used with such effect in some of the *Canterbury Tales*. Troilus, to be sure, laments his woes forcibly and at great length, so much so that some readers have too hastily condescended to him as being nothing but a love-sick boy. What we ought to observe is that we are not stirred to pity by the long speeches, which are indeed sometimes treated with a shade of derisive humor, but by the course of events through which we follow him from his first sight of Criseyde in the temple to his final enlightenment.

Criseyde, as I have already intimated, illustrates Chaucer's tragic pathos so well but in such a different way that we may profitably consider her apart from Troilus. That Chaucer did not intend her to be the central figure is made clear both at the beginning and end of the poem. The "double sorwe" of Troilus is the theme, and at the conclusion the effect upon him of Criseyde's perfidy is what we see, while she has altogether disappeared from view. Yet the second of the five books is largely devoted to her, and elsewhere she is subordinated to Troilus only by the assumption that what happens to him is the main concern. Readers in our time have tended to shift the emphasis, fascinated as we can't help being by Criseyde's mind and heart. It is Chaucer's great triumph that we are convinced of her beauty and captivated by her personal charm even though her weaknesses are never minimized. She rouses our pity not so much because she is sinned against but because, with all her good qualities, she is betrayed by her "slyding corage," her lack of steadfastness, into a perfidy which she herself comprehends and bewails. Chaucer's summary comment upon her points out quite exactly the tragic pathos of her fate.[22]

> And if I myghte excuse hire any wise,
> For she so sory was for hire untrouthe,
> Iwis, I wolde excuse hire yet for routhe.

Chaucer's infallible sense of what we may term the literary proprieties and his consequent choice of the right mood and the means to implement it are strikingly illustrated by the *Franklin's Tale*, which may serve as a final example. The promise of the heroine to give herself to the ingenious and importunate Aurelius was intentionally fantastic on her part but psychologically sound. She was worried about her adventurous and dearly loved husband. Any devoted wife would feel the same anxiety. What follows,

[22] *T&C*, v,1097-1099.

however, flutters on the edge of credibility. The magician's show at Orleans was convincing, but no more than an illusion that the rocks off Brittany had been removed was asked of him. The story thus becomes one of trick and counter trick, with the reader's interest wholly directed on the behavior of Dorigen, her husband, and her suitor. The only reality is in them, and only by sympathy with them can our feelings be stirred. Yet Chaucer did nothing to make them act or speak with the simple naturalness which he knew so well how to assume. Instead, they are kept to a decorous formality. A little reflection convinces one that this treatment of them is perfectly right. The scenes and figures may lack poignancy, but they interpret to us certain aspects of human nature and human behavior with marvellous justice. Pathos would be out of key, even though the three right-minded and sensitive persons involved would have suffered very keenly. We are instructed, but we are not involved. The experience is intellectual, not emotional.

vi · the limitations of chaucer

THE only good reason for exploring the limitations of an admired author is the hope of finding in his work values before unappreciated. If he appears less important as the result of a dispassionate scrutiny, we may be regretful at the loss of an illusion, but we can be satisfied that we have come nearer a just estimate of his worth. We must take pains, be it said, to keep our scrutiny as nearly dispassionate as possible; and we ought to remember that no judgment on a work of art can be of much value if it is made by a dull or indolent mind. The critic is always quite as much on trial as the person or object being tried.

In forming one's estimate it will not do to ignore areas of neglect in thought, or feeling, or expression, pretending that they have no importance. The habits of the ostrich have never been regarded with respect. We cannot help regretting, for example, that Geoffrey Chaucer did not explore the possibilities for poetic expression in the native English verse-forms. His contemporary, the anonymous genius who wrote *Sir Gawain and the Green Knight* and *The Pearl,* as well as the other genius who may with some safety be called William Langland, made good use of the opportunity which Chaucer ignored. Their beautiful and very sophisticated poetry is in a wholly different tradition of craftsmanship from his. The swift flowering of that tradition is one of those literary phenomena which bewilder us because we know so little why men write as they do and what makes them shift from one fashion to another. Studies in literary genetics have not carried us far. About all we can say is that writers sometimes perfect a mode rather suddenly, finding it suitable to their purposes.

The use of alliterative verse and of certain complex stanzaic patterns, both in the native English tradition, had no future of great consequence. In minor ways only did these habits continue to affect our poetry, while the main current was that shared with writers of the Continent. To Chaucer, completely bilingual as it seems certain that he was and belonging to the court circle, there can have been no question of choosing one way or another. It would not have occurred to him to write otherwise than the way he did, and it must be regarded as a fortunate chance that he perfected himself in English rather than French. If conditions, economic and political, had been only a little different, he might easily have vied with his friend Deschamps in Deschamps' own tongue. That he was aware of other fashions than the one to which he adhered we know from evidence which he himself furnished, though the evidence is tantalizingly meagre. In the prologue to the *Parson's Tale* the good priest replies to the Host that he will fulfil his obligations to the company:

> But trusteth wel, I am a Southren man,
> I kan nat geeste 'rum, ram, ruf,' by lettre.[1]

The reference to alliterative verse is plain, though it is a little odd that neither Chaucer nor the Parson knew that by no means all of it was written in the North. As commentators have frequently pointed out, the Parson in the line next following says that he holds rhyme "but litel bettre," which leaves one a little doubtful whether "rum, ram, ruf" implies condescension to the poetry so patterned.[2] There is no doubt, however, about the attitude towards popular poetry exhibited in *Sir Thopas*, which is the most extravagant of burlesques and amusing only because so

[1] *CT*, x,42,43.

[2] The pious note of Skeat that "neither Chaucer himself nor his amiable parson would have spoken slightingly of other men's labours" should be checked in the light of *Sir Thopas*.

many absurdities and inanities are packed into it. It is wholly unsympathetic to the matter and manner of popular romances, and indeed altogether malicious.

We cannot regret, certainly, that Chaucer followed the main stream of literary tradition instead of channels which he might perhaps have done something to establish and keep flowing. English poetry since his day has had a noble history, which owes much to the example he set. Yet his failure to understand the value of what other poets were doing in a different vein must be reckoned one of his limitations. There is no reason to suppose that he would have seen the work of the man who wrote *The Pearl,* and very likely he would have regarded the language of it as barbarous. It is almost certain, I think, that he would have found both *The Pearl* and *Sir Gawain* hard reading if he had encountered them. *Piers Plowman* would not have been difficult, but it would have seemed bucolic. He can hardly have escaped some knowledge of it, one would think, since the number of surviving manuscripts indicate that it was a good deal read.

No one can argue with any confidence that Chaucer would have written even greater poems if he had been responsive to the efforts of some of his contemporaries. What we may be allowed to believe, however, is that his work would have gained intensity of personal feeling if he had been affected by the nationalism which was at least partly responsible for the renewed cultivation of alliterative verse and for the elaborate stanzaic patterns used in plays and romances. Dante's passion for his country did not make him less absorbed in the great themes of the *Divine Comedy.* Chaucer's poetic domain was altogether different, of course, for his thought did not scale the heights nor plumb the depths. The minds and hearts of living men made up the field of his explorations. We must be humbly grateful for his great achievement, acknowledging some limitations of his mind and taste but not apologizing for them or for him. Canst thou draw out leviathan with an hook?

A more downright judgment is possible about another conservative practice of the poet. Although he wrote several very charming descriptions of gardens and forest glades and the feelings inspired by mornings in spring, he gives the reader no impression of something freshly seen, of beauties newly discovered. The various echoes of older poetry which have been noted in the opening lines of the General Prologue[3] do not mean that the passage is imitative, but they emphasize the traditionalism with which Chaucer's treatment of nature is everywhere infused. He did not see it with a fresh eye, but he saw it with its beauty in some ways enhanced. It was charged with the emotions felt by others in many times. Furthermore, the stylization is done with such delicacy that the fact of it may be overlooked. There have been countless readers, I suppose, who have thought such passages as the introduction to the assembly at the Tabard Inn completely simple and unstudied although, as I have intimated, it belongs in a sequence of highly wrought descriptive images.

Equally artificial yet fresh with what seems childlike simplicity is the ritual adoration of the daisy in the prologue of the *Legend of Good Women*.[4] Between the two versions of the passage, which differ from one another considerably in substance and arrangement, there is little to choose, which is a matter of some significance. Nothing could show more clearly that the beauty of the pictured scene was not the result of a spontaneous outpouring of unpremeditated art but something executed with conscious artistry. Chaucer's vision was limited by his traditionalism, if you please, but scarcely to the detriment of his poetry. How he was affected by scenes of natural beauty with which human

[3] Conveniently summarized by Robinson, *Poetical Works*, p. 752.

[4] Version F, lines 107-147; version G, lines 89-133.

imagination had not played we do not know. He furnishes no clue. All in all, he was a poet of the town rather than of the country, a poet to whom nature in the restricted sense was important only as it furnished a setting for men and women. Though it is a matter for rather idle speculation, one must conclude that he would not have found great satisfaction in the romantic beauty of Vaucluse, which to Petrarch a generation earlier had been a happy retreat. In that respect Petrarch was nearer our time than Chaucer.

It would have been not at all consistent with his other attributes if Chaucer had found lyric poetry in its strictest sense a natural mode of self-expression. It would have been equally strange if he had not written the "balades, roundels, virelayes" which Alceste urges in his defence when she reviews his works in the prologue to the *Legend of Good Women*. An aspirant poet in the court circle of Edward III could not have failed to write in that vein, whether using French or English, If any virelayes or roundels made by him have survived, they have never been identified, while the ballades and the other short poems which we know to be his, though they are graceful, give no indication that he had a great gift for song. Certainly he cannot have been one of the poets—some of them in his own century—who have found in the lyric a means of self-revelation. With one exception the most poignantly lyrical utterances in all Chaucer's works are perhaps the song of Troilus, when his resistance to the power of love is on the point of breaking down, and that of Antigone in praise of love as she walks in the palace garden with the very receptive Criseyde.[5] The exception is the address to the Virgin in the prologue to the *Second Nun's Tale*, which is intensely personal yet dependent in phrase and image on the *Paradiso* and various Latin hymns. So much so that in one way (though a false way) of looking at the matter it is scarcely Chaucer's at

[5] *T&C*, I,400-420, II,834-875.

all.[6] Chaucer, we must conclude, did not depend for his greatness on lyrical poetry, though on occasion he wrote magnificently in that vein. The passionate warmth and immediacy which gives us satisfaction in song was not lacking in his work, but it was channelled for the most part in the episodes of narrative.

In view of his masterly accomplishments with verse, one cannot help feeling regret that Chaucer did not give some attention to the improvement of English prose as an instrument. His discovery of the five-measure line in verse as best suited to the natural rhythms of English speech,[7] which has never been long forgotten from that day to this, and his extraordinary virtuosity in the use of the rhymed couplet with lines of that length place him high among our poets who have been skilful craftsmen. The stanza which later came to be known as "rhyme royal" provides another illustration of this. Yet in the use of prose he made no innovations. The *Melibeus,* the *Parson's Tale,* and the *Boece* are pleasant to the ear if read aloud, and "little Lewis" should have found the *Treatise on the Astrolabe* sufficiently clear if he had any scientific aptitude; but they contrast strangely in their somewhat lumbering manner with the finished elegance of the poems. Their style is neither better nor worse than the common run of writings in English prose at the time, though it must be admitted that they are inferior to the exceptional best. A comparison of the *Melibeus* with the French version of the tale is illuminating. In this instance we have a text very close to the one Chaucer translated,[8] and the quality of the prose is in every respect better than Chaucer's. French had already been adapted to a mode of prose utterance which was still very

6 The evidence is most recently summarized in *Sources and Analogues,* pp. 664-667.

7 We should remember that he never went back to using the four-measure line after he adopted the five-measure.

8 See *Sources and Analogues,* pp. 563-565.

uncommon with English. The comparison is worth making if only because it throws into even stronger relief Chaucer's achievements with verse. His limitations in respect of one medium make us realize his greatness as a poet all the more clearly.

A good deal has been said, first and last, about the unspoiled freshness of his verse, moulded from a tongue not yet worn down by careless use. To anyone who has closely examined the poems such a view is wholly inadmissible. No more than Shakespeare did he warble native woodnotes, but on the contrary he was fully aware of his purposes and how to attain them. The freshness is there, but it is not primitivistic. It is there because, like all great poets, Chaucer was master and not captive of the words he used. We cannot take seriously his modest complaint:[9]

> that folk han here-beforn
> Of makyng ropen, and lad awey the corn;
> And I come after, glenynge here and there,
> And am ful glad if I may fynde an ere
> Of any goodly word that they han left.

One cannot agree that he was in any way impoverished or enfeebled by writing as a sophisticated poet in a sophisticated tradition, and it is difficult to believe that he himself thought so. Certainly he did not feel himself hampered by his reliance on earlier "makers" for materials and techniques. The importance of being "original" occurred to no one of course till long after his time.

Another way in which he was consciously limited was personal and would have importance only if he were the mere jester which some persons have thought him rather than the serious-minded artist which better acquaintance shows him to be. He was no reformer. In spite of his keen observation of both the good and the bad, the high and the low in human nature, he had no impulse, it would appear,

[9] *LGW*, Prol. G, 61-65.

to attempt a cure for the follies which were so plain to see. He viewed everything with ironic detachment, seldom expressing indignation on his own part though not infrequently attributing it to characters in some tale he was fashioning and quite as often arousing it in the reader. Sometimes the moral emphasis is strengthened by the seemingly tolerant acceptance of conditions as they are. In reading the *Pardoner's Tale*, for example, our shudders are not induced by the confused sermonizing of the scandalous narrator but by the closely articulated action. The infamous trio who find the death they seek, it is necessary to observe, are not the rioters of the tavern against whom the Pardoner expresses such violent indignation in the tale he begins but quickly abandons.[10] One might say with justice that Chaucer did not allow the drama of the Pardoner's performance to smother the moral force of his fable.

For Chaucer was a sound moralist though no reformer. His attitude cannot be better defined than in his own words of advice to a friend, possibly Sir Philip de la Vache.[11]

> Tempest thee noght al croked to redresse,
> In trust of hir that turneth as a bal.

Since in the order of the world Fortune has her established place, and deals directly with human affairs, it is idle to believe that everything crooked can be put straight, no matter how attempted. It is then foolish for the individual to storm and fret because he cannot do so. Such reasoned acquiescence in things as they are does not mean approval. But it is a sensible view to adopt, though not heroic. That it was Chaucer's own seems to be indicated by what he wrote and by what we know about his life. We may be very grateful that his temperament and inclination permitted him through some decades of national disturbance to make certain great poems.

[10] See p. 64 above.

[11] Usually known as *Truth*, though *Balade de bon Conseyl* is a better title. Lines 8, 9.

Yet there are always the "retractions" to upset our conclusions about him, whatever they may be. There is no doubt that Chaucer wrote the strange apology appended to the *Parson's Tale.* It was accepted by the copyists who put together the manuscripts of the *Canterbury Tales* not so long after the poet died, and we know that in the fifteenth century a story was circulating about his repentance when close to death. This may perhaps be the explanation of one singularly incoherent statement. "And many another book, if they were in my remembrance," he says or is made to say, though all the major works have been mentioned, as well as the unknown *Book of the Lion.* And why, when referring to works pleasing to Heaven, should "othere bookes of legendes of seintes, and omelies, and moralitee" be lumped together without titles? There, I think, we must leave the matter.

All in all, a survey of Chaucer's limitations leaves him in the company of the very great, whatever he may have felt in some hour of weakness. On no account did he need to make excuses for anything he had written, nor need we apologize for him five centuries and a half later. We should be glad, of course, if he had found time to complete some of the projects he left unfinished. We know from *Troilus and Criseyde* that he was capable of shaping a poem of complexity to structural perfection. He was cut off all too soon, and like Shakespeare he was much occupied with worldly affairs because he managed them well. Yet it is not unreasonable to believe that he enjoyed his expeditions as envoy of the King and found some pleasure, too, in looking out for the monarch's palaces and forests.

> Busied about shows of no earthly importance?

Kipling asked concerning another great craftsman, and answered wisely:

> Yes, but he knew it!

KEY TO ABBREVIATIONS

CHAUCER'S WORKS

BD	*The Book of the Duchess*
CT	*The Canterbury Tales*
HF	*The House of Fame*
Lady	*A Complaint to his Lady*
LGW	*The Legend of Good Women*
Mars	*The Complaint of Mars*
PF	*The Parliament of Fowls*
T&C	*Troilus and Criseyde*

JOURNALS AND TEXTS

ASS	*Acta Sanctorum*
EETS	*Publications of the Early English Text Society*
JEGP	*Journal of English and Germanic Philology*
MGH	*Monumenta Germaniae Historica*
MLN	*Modern Language Notes*
MLQ	*Modern Language Quarterly*
MLR	*Modern Language Review*
MP	*Modern Philology*
PMLA	*Publications of the Modern Language Association of America*
PQ	*Philological Quarterly*